Thoughts from s
deep breath and turned the page.

*"It is deeply moving but not trite and answers
questions I didn't even realise I had about dying.
I cried, laughed and it made me
assess my own relationships."*

*"It made me want to spend some wine-
fuelled evenings with the Curtains."*

*"This is a love story. I feared that my own
experience of loss would make reading about the
intimacy of dying too painful but it is done in
a way that I actually found comforting."*

*"I love reading books you just can't put
down and this was one of them!"*

*"It's like a two-way experience. An extraordinary
feeling and I felt healing for my own grief.
That's quite an achievement."*

*"I never reread books but I know there will be a
time when I will want to reread this one."*

*"It had me sucked in from the very beginning
and I read it like a speeding train."*

"I am heading out to buy myself a new lipstick today."

What will I wear to your funeral?

Kellie Curtain

About the Author

Kellie Curtain is a mother of four and has a degree in nothing but may well hold a Masters in Procrastination. An Australian former television news reporter with a passion for telling other people's stories, she never imagined that if there indeed was a book inside of her it would be about the death of her best friend, her mother.

This wasn't a search for inner peace or a deeper meaning to anything; the first words were written one night after the wine and excuses ran out.

The story itself is not unique; the dialogue however is a little different and it may just start a conversation that many are fearful to have.

Names have not been changed to protect identities, most have simply been left out in the interests of not mentioning one act of kindness or friendship over another – they were all special.

 MIDDLE PAGE
PUBLISHING

Published by Middle Page Publishing
www.middlepagepublishing.com

First published in 2017
www.indeliblemarks.net

A catalogue record for this book is available from the National Library
of Australia.

Cover design and illustration by Karen Greenberg.

ISBN:
978-0-6480436-0-7 (AMZ)
978-0-6480436-1-4 (ING)
978-0-6480436-6-9 (e-bk)

For
Roberto, Stevonovitch and Mick the Dick

From Miss Piggy
With love

x x x

Yesterday is history, tomorrow a mystery, today is a gift.
Eleanor Roosevelt

Prologue

It came just as I knew it would but not when I was expecting it, my new kind of normal.

The beach house that we'd rented in Far North Queensland required a long day of travel from our home in Melbourne, where it was still cold despite it officially being spring. My husband and I walked out onto the balcony that overlooked the sea as our four children ran down the back steps that ended in the sand, and already we felt the trek had been worth it. There was nothing much to do here but after the events of the last six weeks a whole lot of 'nothing' was what we needed.

The sun had begun to fall behind the sea with a magnificent orange hue. We grabbed a bottle of red and two glasses and strolled out to the foreshore. I had plonked sweet baby James on the sand beside us and was laughing at the 'Kodak' moment of our little girls dancing on the water's edge of the mile-long beach, which was all but deserted. They skipped and cartwheeled as the pretty cotton nightdresses Nana had made them mushroomed in the wind, three mops of hair blowing in all directions as they laughed and chased each other.

I was smiling at them, enjoying the glimpse of sibling harmony, when my new normal snuck up on me as suddenly as the waves they were trying to outrun. It was the realisation that I had no one to call.

Never again would someone be waiting for me to phone, wondering if I had got to where I was going, wanting to know I had arrived safely, because that's what mothers do. That's what my mother did and she was gone.

The ritual of ringing Mum to let her know I was safe began in early adolescence and it was non-negotiable. Even at forty years old with children of my own it continued, especially when it involved long travel. I would ring her and debrief with trivial pieces of information, mostly about the children: who was the best behaved, who was testing my patience, who bit whom. This would be followed by a description of what the accommodation was like, the weather, and which night my bins needed putting out at home: all the stuff that no one is really interested in hearing; no one but your mother.

And so there it was, picture-perfect setting shattered, triggered by the void of a single phone call. The heavy weight of reality was tangible, as if my mother had at that very moment dropped dead in front of me. It had been three weeks since her death but it was a defining moment that I hadn't expected. The permanency of her absence was revealed for the first time and it was a loneliness I could never have imagined.

I'd lost my father a few weeks shy of my twenty-second birthday after he died from a heart attack. Even though I was grown, I was now officially an orphan. I was no longer somebody's daughter.

I picked up my phone anyway and punched in the name of one of my brothers. It rang just a few times and was then answered with a familiar and laidback 'Hiii'.

Ceremony isn't our family's strong point. Growing up with three brothers required rough and tumble; we're definitely more the 'call a spade a shovel' kind. My brother knew who was calling so I skipped the formalities of asking how he was and launched straight into my reason for ringing.

'Hi. Look, I know you probably don't give a toss but it's just occurred to me that I have no one to call and let them know we have arrived safely, so I'm ringing you.'

And with just the right amount of humour came the reply: 'You're right! I don't give a toss,' and he began to laugh. 'But I'm glad that you have arrived safely. How is your place?' And the conversation continued.

Life without the family lynchpin was going to take a lot of getting used to, I knew that, though it was the little things that were catching me off guard and having the most impact. Finding one of her lipsticks in my bag would simultaneously console and crush me. I had applied more bright lipstick in the last few weeks than in my entire life.

We opened a second bottle of red on the balcony that night as we sat listening to the ocean. We had booked the holiday seven months ago and I'd asked Mum to come with us but she'd declined the offer. I'm sure she had a sixth sense of what was going to happen; she always did.

The next morning I woke early to the loud and joyous sounds of wildlife. Lying in bed looking through the window I spotted two kookaburras perched proudly on the balcony railing. There was no trademark laughing. Their heads made small staccato movements as they peered through the glass into the room next to mine. They appeared to be observing the children, who were already up and playing.

Moments later a text came through from my big brother. It simply said, 'No kookaburras today.' In the days since Mum had been gone he hadn't said much at all, but I knew instantly what the three-word message meant.

It was a reference to a pair of the native birds that had been coming to his backyard on the Victoria coast every morning since Mum died. He was certain they were the same two that he and Mum had been feeding months before. They would come first thing in the morning and occasionally return in the afternoon or if it rained. If no one was outside when they arrived they would wait – they knew eventually someone would come out with a slice of meat and would happily take food from their hands.

The thought that somehow Mum was connected to the birds I was looking at was ridiculous and yet I couldn't help but take a strange comfort. On the first day the kookas didn't pay my brother a visit I had two looking through our lounge window.

I texted back: 'No, the kookaburras aren't with you today because they are with me, it's Mum checking to see I am safe.'

Sometime in the 70s

$\int$tudying every move, *I would gaze upward and watch. She would pucker her lips and expertly guide the lipstick tip from one corner across the bow to the other side. Her mouth would then open a little more and she would stretch her lips into a stiff smile, glide the bold colour across the bottom lip from one side to the other then back again for good measure and then she would always rub her lips together.*

There were so many different shades in her collection, more than anyone would need yet she would buy more, even duplicates of her favourites, although she was also eager to try something new. Her preference was for those with a 'blue' base, though it took me years to understand what that meant. There was a drawer full of them and every single one was Revlon. It was a lifelong loyalty; she insisted every other brand made her 'itch'.

She was never fully dressed until lipstick had been applied. One to match every outfit, even mixing them to get the colour just right, and over time each one would be moulded to an arch shape with a pointy tip.

The ladies' magazines revealed that where the user had created a pointy tip to their lipsticks, this signified someone who was adventurous, complex and would make a great detective. She was certainly adventurous when it came to lipstick shades, though there was no room in her drawer for token tints or barely there colours.

Who knew there could be so many different colours? She did. Who would remember the quirky names that separated one hue from another? She would! Wine with Everything, Kiss me Coral, Sly Red, Plumalicious, she was partial to any that had a shimmer effect.

Even if she wasn't leaving the house she had lipstick on. Every bag, and she had a closet of those too, had a few rolling around inside and there were also several on standby in the car console. A fresh coat of lipstick signalled that she was armed and ready for anything or nothing in particular, it was never too early to reapply and a mirror was not essential. Driving along, eyes still on the road, with one hand she'd ease the top off a lipstick cylinder, place it between her teeth and twist it around once to reveal the wax stick. A quick once-over across the top lip, a swipe across the bottom, then the lip rub and it was done, she was ready.

She wore Sandstorm

May 2009

The phone was answered with a cheery 'Heeello', though she knew exactly who it would be.

'Hi, Mum. How did the scan go?'

I knew she had a girlfriend over for dinner but I wanted to ask how her mammogram went because she hadn't been feeling a hundred per cent for a few weeks and her GP just wanted to make sure. No big deal, 'old age', they guessed, though at sixty-nine she didn't look or feel old.

'It was fine but I have to go back next week as they didn't do it properly.'

'OK, great, speak to you tomorrow.'

I had started to flick through the TV channels when I replayed her answer in my head and realised I'd heard that line before. I immediately grabbed the phone and pressed redial.

'What did they find?'

Quick as a whip but in a nonchalant manner she replied, 'Nothing! It just has to be done again.'

I reminded her that she'd used that excuse on another occasion when she didn't want to cause alarm; the split-second pause betrayed her.

'Oh,' signalled her surrender, and she knew I was onto her.

Whether it was my pregnancy hormones in overdrive or a sixth sense, in that moment I knew it was going to be bad. I started to cry whilst Mum sat helpless on the other end of the phone. She was trying to keep calm and not let on to her friend that something was wrong as she made a futile attempt to reassure me. 'We won't know anything until next week.'

I hung up the phone, rested my head on the table and sobbed.

A few days later it was Mother's Day. The line-up for lunch included my three brothers, their wives, and six children under six. Anywhere our family gathered was where Mum was happiest – it had always been that way – and the banter was as fluid as the wine being poured. But it didn't take long before Mum addressed the elephant in the room. 'I just want to tell you all that if it's cancer I'm not having treatment.'

'Like hell you're not!' was the collective response, though no one spoke. The silence wasn't because we were lost for words – our family is never lost for words. The quiet moment was nothing more than a gesture of respect for the matriarch before we began the gentle assault on her no-treatment position.

'Let's just wait and see what the doctor says this week,' said one of my brothers in an effort to break the lull in conversation, but Mum was having none of it. 'I'm not going through that again.'

The word 'again' slapped us with a stark reminder of how much we didn't know the first time she had battled the disease.

I was fifteen when Mum was first diagnosed with breast cancer; old enough to know that death was possible, and yet I don't remember ever fearing that she would die. 'It will all be fine,' Mum had said, and she was usually right. Everything remained as it had been and for the most part I have no memory of anything being out of the ordinary apart from her having a few days in hospital to have the 'lump' cut out. We had been told that she'd have chemotherapy, and a very expensive wig was made in preparation for her hair loss, but it never fell out, which served as a fortuitous diversion from the seriousness of her condition. The radiotherapy left nasty burns and scars on the skin under her arm but she played that down too so the impact on us was almost nil. What we did notice was the sudden addition of soy milk, dairy-free butter spread and yeast-free bread to the fridge, but not much thought was given to the reason why. How blissfully ignorant we were.

Every year Mum had quietly celebrated the call that gave her the all-clear, but as the five- and ten-year milestones passed, the clean bill of health never really seemed a reason to break out the champagne – rather they were marked by a chorus of 'Good to hear, Mum'. After more than two decades of her being cancer free we arrogantly assumed that Mum had well and truly won her fight. Clearly she hadn't. It was back.

As our Mother's Day lunch wrapped up there were none of the usual arguments over whose turn it was to clean up; everyone was looking for a distraction, even if it meant clearing the dishes. The grandchildren were oblivious to the dark cloud looming over our family, and their light-hearted antics and toddler squabbles kept the mood from plummeting, but I was suddenly preoccupied with the thought of the frightening knock to her mortality she'd shouldered all those years ago, the prospect of leaving behind four children, the youngest of whom was only four at the time.

Lying in bed that night I was kept awake by visions of two decades before that I had never actually been exposed to. I wept for my mother and what must have been a crushing loneliness as she put her own rest and recovery aside because her priority was to shelter my brothers and me from the vomiting, fatigue and other painful side effects of her treatment. But I also cried tears of shame at not properly acknowledging her annual victories, which had eventually clocked up twenty-four years.

When I collected Mum for her oncologist's appointment the following morning she was waiting for me on her front veranda dressed in a smart warm coat to keep out the May chill, her short hair coiffed and perfect make-up. My mother was beautiful to look at; I was biased but I could tell from the way others admired her. A petite five-foot-two blonde with ice-blue eyes, her facial features were in perfect proportion, with a slightly imperfect nose. The skin on her face was like silk although almost everywhere else she had suffered the effects of a lifetime of itching stemming from childhood eczema that never left; her hands were badly scarred and she was forever embarrassed by them. She didn't like her teeth either. In just about every picture she would hide them behind her perfect lips that were a flawless canvas for a bold or bright lipstick. That morning they were painted in a deep, rich, somewhat serious 'don't mess with me' colour, which might have been Rum 'n' Raisin.

The twenty-minute journey was filled with conversation about the kids and a debrief of the family gathering the day before. As we neared our destination she issued a reminder: 'Now, I've told you, I don't care what the prognosis is, I'm not having chemotherapy!'

'OK, OK,' I said defensively, but in truth I was not even a little bit 'OK' with her stance. I knew Mum wanted me to support her decision, to present a united front, but my need to have her alive was greater. Of course I didn't want her to suffer unnecessarily but if the gain from any pain was to have her around for a few more years then I wanted her to fight.

The doctor had come highly recommended though she was younger than we had expected. My bulging belly, incubating my fourth child, was an easy conversation starter; she was also a mother of young children. Opening the file the oncologist looked down at her notes. 'So, Pamela ...'

I felt compelled to take the pause hostage. 'It's not good, is it?'

It was a knee-jerk reaction to demonstrate that we didn't need a gentle delivery of bad news.

'No,' the doctor confessed. She explained that the tests couldn't determine if it was the original cancer returned for an encore more than two decades later or a new breast cancer. Contemplating the how and why was irrelevant; the cancer had advanced and spread to her liver.

I cut to the chase. 'Can it be cured?'

'No,' was the gentle but firm answer. The doctor proceeded to explain possible treatments that could slow down the progression of the disease when Mum interrupted. 'No thank you, been there done that. Never again!'

'I understand,' the doctor said sympathetically. 'But you would be amazed at how much chemotherapy has changed.'

We sat and listened to the options that would only delay the inevitable. Mum looked unconvinced and no more receptive to the idea regardless of medical advancements. There was only question that hung in the air. I grabbed it and threw it abruptly into the mix of medical options. 'How long does Mum have?'

My sensible self knew that despite the oncologist's experience and expertise she didn't have a crystal ball, and the answer was going to be an educated guess but one we would hang off anyway. 'With treatment a year to eighteen months.'

'Without treatment?' I asked.

Her response was immediate. 'Six months.'

Despite the careful and considered delivery the verdict was a complete shock and felt brutal. Even Mum looked stunned that death's door was so close.

In another impulsive reaction I reached for black humour. 'Geez, Mum, bet you're glad you gave up the whisky a year ago, fat load of good that did! It was probably keeping the cancer at bay.'

'On the contrary,' the doctor interrupted with a serious tone. 'Cutting the alcohol out is probably why she is still here.' She turned her full attention to Mum. 'Pamela, perhaps you could just give it a try? You can stop at any time.'

The 'OK' I had given Mum in the car to refuse chemotherapy was, in my mind, already null and void, there was simply no other effective option on offer.

I bit my tongue and hoped I wouldn't have to beg her to try. Mum inhaled a deep breath and then looked at me. 'OK,' she said.

The war against cancer was to start first thing the next day and despite the lack of conviction in Mum's response I grabbed the baton of hope and charged ahead. Already I was feeling buoyed and began to think of researching supplementary ways to beat the odds. As the doctor walked us to the door, I wanted to know if there was any way, short of a miracle, that Mum could expect to live longer than a year. 'So if the treatment is positive and works well, what could we be looking at?'

'About eighteen months, maybe two years,' she said.

I was caught off guard that the best scenario wasn't really very good at all. 'That's it? Do many people go past two years?' I asked, pressing the specialist to look closer into the non-existent crystal ball for any glimmer of hope that might turn the bleak and black future into a shade of grey.

Her tone was kind and warm but the answer was the same. 'No.' And once again she turned and redirected her focus to Mum. 'You are feeling well now, Pamela, and hopefully you will for most days in between treatments but if there are things you have been wanting to do, now is the time.'

As we walked into the mid-morning sun carrying a virtual death sentence, I felt a seismic shift. From the moment I was born it had been my mother protecting and caring for me but in the space of an hour our lives had been irrevocably altered and the roles would soon be reversed.

Six months. It was worse than either of us had expected. If Mum had been told that with no treatment she might have one good year left then I was certain she'd have walked away from medical intervention, but six months? She wouldn't even see Christmas! It was glaringly obvious to me and I reasoned to myself that it was equally clear to Mum that there was no choice but to accept the doctor's recommendation, though my rationale didn't prevent the guilt I suddenly felt, as if I had somehow betrayed her. An hour earlier I had agreed that there would be no chemotherapy, the decision had to be hers; I knew I had to give Mum a way out.

'Listen. If you are happy to tell me that you're comfortable with having celebrated your last Mother's Day and your last Christmas then we will cancel the appointment for tomorrow.'

It was a high-risk strategy. What the hell was I going to do if she took the 'out'? Thankfully she didn't but there was one condition she insisted was not up for negotiation. 'I'm going to try. I'm not worried about losing my hair, but if my quality of life is no good I might as well be dead. I promise you that I'm going to give it my best but I want you to promise me that when I say "I've had enough" then that's it.'

Oh sure, I thought to myself; Mum wanted me to agree to sign off on her death, and I couldn't do that. It would be OK for her if she was dead, but it would be me left behind. I didn't have it in me to honour such a deal – I was too selfish. How could I ever make such a promise? But I was mentally dealing with one figurative bushfire at a time. 'Agreed.' I nodded, knowing full well I was lying.

She wore Fire and Ice

Death had never been a taboo subject in our family; even when I was a young child death was never sugarcoated or dismissed as something not to worry about. 'Dying is a part of life,' Mum would say, and she never dressed it up as anything more than, 'We all have to die some day.'

My father was a thoroughbred-horse trainer and on weekend mornings after he'd gone to supervise early-morning track work I'd crawl into my parents' bed next to Mum for a cuddle and chat. Every so often I would notice her staring out of the window, quite visibly locked in a moment. Whenever I asked what she was thinking the reply would be 'my mother'. Little Nana, as we had called her, had died in her sleep when I was five but I grew to recognise those reflective pauses; they diminished over the years but never ceased.

The harsh reality of death had hit our family on the cusp of my twenty-second birthday when my father died from a heart attack; the man with a large six-foot-two frame and larger-than-life personality simply dropped dead at the racetrack one afternoon. To the uninitiated death is a concept hard to grasp. Parents, regardless of age, somehow seem immortal. There was no warning when Dad bent down to tighten the girth on one of his horses. The stablehand noticed Dad leaning against the animal and asked him if he was OK. There was no reply. It was quiet and quick.

Dad had cheated death on two other occasions with heart attacks that should have killed him. The near-miss experiences provided a short-term wake-up call to take better care of himself but long term did little to curb his love of too much food, wine and a secret but well-known affair with tobacco. From the age of sixteen I started to guard myself against his medically predicted demise, especially when I knew he didn't expect to prove the experts wrong. He insisted that my twenty-first birthday party be a big event – much bigger than I had expected or wanted. When the night arrived he told me why: 'I'm not going to be around to see you get married.'

Almost a year later, on the morning that would turn out to be his last, he stomped down the hallway after growling at me about something. I laughed to myself that the man supposedly living on borrowed time might outlive us all and indulged in a fleeting thought that he could even be around long enough to walk me down an aisle. A few hours later he was dead.

Even though his demise wasn't a complete shock it was sudden and we hadn't prepared ourselves. There were no poignant words, just 'bye'.

Dad's life in the racing industry had required him to work seven days a week, and the term work also included the social aspect. In fact, Dad just loved being social: whether it was friends or family he was the life of the party until he would inevitably fall asleep in a corner chair. Known for his big heart, big laugh and humour, everyone wanted a piece of him. During my childhood he was very much the authoritative figure, but 4.30-am starts and late finishes made him largely absent. He never did typical dad things like take out the rubbish bins or mow the lawns; there was not a 'snowball's chance in hell' of him attending a parent-teacher interview let alone helping with homework or ferrying kids to sports games. Mum did all of that. The only common ground we seemed to share with other families was watching *The Wonderful World of Disney* on Sunday nights, eating toasted sandwiches with a side of Heinz canned tomato soup.

When he died I had been living back at home for ten months. A job retrenchment had put the brakes on my finances and ability to pay rent. During that time I was working a few casual jobs and Dad had begun spending a little less time at race meets during the week. Mum was busy running her florist shop, which she had opened a few years earlier, and Dad and I would watch the odd midday movie together. He was forever a receptive audience for my cooking and we were closer than we'd ever been.

The cards of sympathy and heartfelt letters continued to fill our mailbox for about eight weeks but eventually petered out, and it was then that our family really began to feel the loneliness of death. For my older brother Robert, who didn't live at home, it was the absence of a daily phone call from Dad that hurt. Their closeness had only really developed in recent years but 'Roberto', as Dad had nicknamed him as a young boy, enjoyed a few precious years that my younger brothers didn't. Stephen was almost a mirror image of his father's lovable larrikin personality, though he'd only just begun to harness their kinship when death cut it short. Dubbed 'Stevonovitch' by Dad as a boy, he was still happily washing his old man's car each week even in his twenties, although I suspect a disproportionate amount of money changed hands. Dad enjoyed tipping everyone and anyone more than was expected and at all times made sure his children had money in their pockets 'just in case'. As for my youngest brother Michael, he was only eleven when Dad died, old enough to have accrued the nickname 'Mick the dick' but there hadn't been nearly enough time for a boy to create sufficient memories of his father.

The brutal veracity of death would hit at random times as we adjusted to life without Dad's loud voice and large presence. I found myself missing the Saturday race-day routine when the radio was switched to the racing station and the phone would ring all morning. I missed the smell of horsehair on clothes in the laundry, and his shower-and-shaving ritual that included perfectly pitched whistling and singing, and I missed seeing the suit and tie and freshly ironed shirt that Mum used to lay out on the bed for him. It felt somewhat unfair that the world had moved on whilst we hadn't and in many ways didn't want to. Mum's days were kept busy with her shop but it was the nights and the empty side of the bed she couldn't escape. I noticed she took to putting pillows down Dad's side, and it became a habit she never broke.

She wore Spiced Brandy

Living with cancer became familiar very quickly: the road down to oncology; the nurses; other cancer patients.

I went to every doctor's appointment with Mum. If she was prepared to fight cancer I wanted to stand right alongside her. There were also other reasons I insisted on being there: it eased the pressure on Mum to remember everything discussed; I asked questions that she hadn't thought of or had forgotten; but most importantly I wanted to hear everything for myself, because Mum couldn't be trusted. Given half the chance I knew she would fail to relay any bad news or at the very least attempt to dilute it.

We would sit in various waiting rooms looking around at other patients, careful not to make unwanted eye contact. We constantly reminded ourselves that she should consider herself lucky. At almost seventy she could reflect on what had been a happy marriage and four healthy children who had become happy adults and whom she'd seen marry. In her late forties after sixteen years as a stay-at-home mum she'd resumed her career as a florist, opened a new shop and built it into a successful business that supported her when she was widowed, then happily sold it to spend maximum time being a nana. Cancer could have robbed her of much of that if it had won the first round more than two decades ago. My grateful thoughts were fleeting though and soon gave way to selfish ones. What about all those I knew who had both parents? Their children had both sets of grandparents. My children had one living grandparent; when she was gone that would be it.

Even more than that, it was about me. I was painfully aware that all my eggs were in her basket and had been for so long that not even she could really grasp that. Yes, she had experienced the heartache of losing her mother, to whom she was very close, but she also had three sisters; I had none. I'd been blessed with amazing girlfriends and three wonderful sisters-in-law, but it's not the same. She was it and I was about to lose her.

Behind the clinical white doors of oncology were first names and friendly conversations and before long light-hearted jokes and dry humour, strangers finding comfort in others on the same journey. The leather recliner chairs that lined either side of the oncology ward created an unlikely catwalk lined with patients in brightly coloured beanies or scarves. As we walked it we were met with cheery greetings of, 'Morning, Pamela.' I would leave knowing she was happy and in safe hands until she was ready to be collected.

Never one to play the victim or wallow in despair at her fate, Mum was soon buying cakes to take to the nursing staff and fellow patients. Determined to stay useful and keep busy, she took on small projects with a purpose and a focus other than herself. One morning I arrived to pick her up for treatment and along with her overnight bag were floral arrangements she'd whipped up in her kitchen to donate to a fundraiser for the breast-cancer nurses. I helped her take the creations into the church hall where the small event was being held and watched her place them into position and complete a final tweak, then walk across the road to the hospital for her chemotherapy. It gave her joy and satisfaction knowing that she was in some small way helping those who were helping her.

The wards and waiting rooms were full of people feeling bad; my mother was one of them and yet she wasn't.

The pills had autonomy over what happened on the inside but she still had a say in how they affected her on the outside.

When I feel like crap the only thing I want to wear are things that bring me comfort, starting with the undies your mother warns you not to be wearing in case you get hit by a bus, and include track pants and sloppy tops. It means no washing and blow-drying hair, no colour coordination of outfits, no accessories of any sort, nor make-up, and certainly no bright lipstick. But Mum would front up to every treatment and appointment in her version of battle armour. It was a mindset: she had always taken pride in her appearance and she wasn't about to stop. It wasn't killer heels and designer threads but rather a stylish smart-casual outfit and without fail a 'statement' lipstick.

As the weeks passed Mum became more concerned with the women whose stories were much worse than her own, especially the younger ones. We would cross paths with a couple of them in the hospital coffee shop. Some were in their thirties with young children at home to care for, and again I was reminded of what my mother had been through twenty-five years ago. She could relate to those women and the worries they carried not for themselves, but for their children. It was indeed a reason to see our glass as half full even if it was for a fleeting moment, and to be honest it was fleeting as I resumed my focus of worrying more about my own pending loss.

Fears related to the cancer treatment had for the most part been fuelled by the unknown but they began to fade as drips, blood tests and a dispensary of pills became part of our routine. The only exceptions were result days. Every few weeks a blood sample would be taken and analysed to assess what effect the treatment was having on the tumours in Mum's liver. A drop in the marker numbers was a 'win' for hope: it would mean the treatment was working and offer the chance of a reprieve. No change in the markers was better than nothing or at least indicated that things were stable, but a rise in the markers wasn't good and it would signal that the tumours were growing and that we needed to try something new.

Those damn markers became the Holy Grail. We followed the doctors' recommended course of action whilst I researched holistic approaches to support the conventional, and eagerly committed health sin 101 by consulting Dr Google. Mum bought a fancy juicer and started making raw-vegetable mocktails with fresh ginger and anything else I discovered that might have healing properties. Turmeric kept coming up as the big herb of hope. Not only was it supposed to fight cancer, it was good for Mum's arthritis. Throw in the added benefit of boosting one's memory and I needed no further convincing to add the orange spice to everything. 'Let me guess, it has turmeric,' Mum would say of a dish that had the telltale orange-brown hue. The taste was subtle and Mum didn't mind, or perhaps it was more that she didn't mind humouring me. Fresh black pepper was also liberally sprinkled on food because I'd read that it increased the effect of the turmeric, and I grasped at the magic nutrients of tomatoes. Daily pots of strong black tea made in the grand silver Robur teapot that had weathered so many personal storms were produced, and alternated with the wonders of white pearls of jasmine, and I couldn't resist buying vitamins despite the slim chance of being able to change the course of a fast-looming fate. I was constantly on the lookout for anything available. I read books on healing that had failed for friends but which I hoped would somehow work for us. There was a never-ending list of things to try: someone who knew someone who'd had success.

I knew it was possible, even probable, that my extra efforts would not make one ounce of difference to the outcome or give her one extra day, but 'maybe' was a reason to give anything a go. I felt that it was a bit like

31

taking lotto numbers: it's a fact that the odds of losing are far greater than winning but it doesn't stop thousands of people including me buying tickets. And anyway, as long as my farfetched optimism didn't compromise the medical approach I figured we had nothing to lose. The cure for cancer would be found one day; who was to say it wouldn't be within our timeframe?

Despite Mum's steely determination and medical advancements nothing could stop some of the side effects that followed each session of chemotherapy.

In her first encounter with cancer in the mid-1980s she had defied the odds somewhat by not losing her hair. The stylish blonde wig she'd had made never even came out of the tissue paper; that same piece had since become a well-worn item in my children's dress-up box. In our initial meeting with the oncologist she had warned Mum, 'Your hair will fall out.'

'That's what they said last time,' Mum had replied with a slight smirk on her face, but the doctor reiterated with certainty: 'It *will* fall out.'

'When it starts to fall out, I will just shave it off,' Mum had said with defiance.

It seemed strange to be going shopping for a wig when Mum still had hair but she wanted to be prepared. The small narrow wig shop in the middle of the outer suburbs was empty when we arrived, and the bell on the door rang loudly as we entered. A petite woman welcomed us to look around and then stepped back; she was clearly used to allowing the clientele to set the level of engagement. Whilst not everyone who came in search of a wig would be a cancer patient, most were.

The ice was broken as we both began trying on wigs. At times I had wondered what I'd look like with black hair; I discovered it wasn't flattering. We giggled at the prospect of her never having to blow-dry or style, just set and forget! My mother was trying on pixie cuts and other short styles in an array of colours: chestnut, auburn and blonde. It was a novel exercise but none allowed her to really look like herself.

The store woman was amazing in her knowledge and guidance as we were steered back towards a style more in keeping with Mum's current blonde ear-length layered style. She placed one hand on Mum's head, began 'foofing' and 'poofing' it as if it was her own hair, and the synthetic imposter instantly looked effortlessly natural. But amongst the positive and fun vibe we had created, and despite our success in finding the perfect piece, I noticed a sadness flash across Mum's face. It lasted only a second as she looked at her reflection in the cubicle mirror, as if catching the grim realisation of the road she knew she was now on. The reality, however harsh, wasn't enough to stop her returning to the shop a few weeks later to support a friend of mine who'd been diagnosed with breast cancer, albeit with a much better prognosis.

Until Mum's hair began to fall out there was still a small way to deny what was happening: we could delay telling my three little girls about their nana. I could fudge if they weren't seeing her one day because she was busy or not feeling well, but how would I explain her bald head? She was very active with them. They were constantly cuddling up to her, often all of them at once. What if in the rough and tumble or on a sleepover the wig came off? How much did they need to know?

She wore Crystal Cut Coral

There was no containing my mother's excitement the day I gave her a small wooden photo frame on which I had painted the word 'Nana' across the top, and in the picture insert were the words 'Coming December 2002'. It was long-awaited news: at last she was to become a grandmother. I'd been married almost four years and I had been enjoying my career as a television news reporter, and whilst Mum never said a word I knew she was forever wondering when she might get grandchildren. I had sworn her to secrecy until the vital twelve-week mark but that didn't stop her buying clothes and indulging in visions of her future role as a grandparent.

Chronic nausea was my reassurance that things were on the right track, but added to the shock and grief when at the eleven-week scan no heartbeat was detected. Worse still, the comforting arms of my mother were not within reach. She had gone on holiday with a girlfriend – her first overseas trip in ten years. Mum was the person I needed most but I couldn't bring myself to tell her, as I knew she would jump on the first plane home and I didn't want that, especially when there was nothing she could do. She'd tell me later that for some unexplained reason she'd felt something was wrong and had stopped buying baby things.

The empty 'Nana' frame was placed in a drawer along with Mum's glorybox for the baby we would never know. Minor complications dragged out into months of annoying procedures and delay in being able to try to fall pregnant again. Mentally and emotionally exhausted I decided on a break from the focus of procreating, though spontaneous tears of loss would still sprout months later. My mother's understanding and willingness to repeatedly hear feelings of frustration was limitless. Her first pregnancy had also ended in miscarriage and she resisted the temptation to encourage me to 'try again', or 'get over it'.

Six months later I gave my mother the green light to get excited again. 'When I become a grandmother I will sell the shop and become a full-time nana,' and three months after McKenzie Mary entered the world that's exactly what she did.

A few days after becoming a mother for the first time I vividly remember sitting on the couch with my baby girl and raging hormones, wondering who was going to hand me the manual to go with the child, when I burst into tears. I cried big heaving sobs as I experienced an unexpected moment of clarity. The magnitude of responsibility and duty of care bestowed on a mother suddenly dawned on me and I realised the monstrous investment and sacrifices the good ones make. I'd known I had a good mother but it was at that moment I truly appreciated that I'd been blessed with an exceptional one. It wasn't that I had been an ungrateful child, it was just one of those scenarios where you don't know until you know, and the words Mum had said to me so many times growing up rang true: 'You won't know until you're a mother.' Countless times during youth and early adult years I had rolled my eyes when I heard her say it but all of a sudden I knew – well, I was just beginning to. In an instant I was in complete awe of my mother as glimpses of my past and future weighed heavily.

'There is no feeling quite like it. Are you just bursting with love?' she had gushed, cupping her first grandchild, soaking in the newborn smell as if inhaling the elixir of true happiness.

I smiled, but not because I was bursting with the love she was talking about; for me that would come later than I expected. My happiness was mirroring hers because I'd never seen my mother so content and joyous. We had always been close – I was the only daughter – but our bond became even stronger and from then on I would see her at least once a day and speak to her first thing in the morning after my husband had left for work, maybe earlier if I'd had a bad night with the children. We'd also talk several times during the day and after the kids had gone to bed. She was the only one to ever ring on the home phone; I'd pick up the receiver and not even need to say hello, I'd just start talking.

There had been a time before having children that I would ring her at 7.10 every morning, the call her alarm clock for work. Sometimes we would chat for five minutes, other times it was twenty-five minutes. One day out of the blue she told me to stop. 'I don't want you to ring me at the same time every day, ring me at different times.' The reason was simple: she had phoned her own mother at the same time each day until one morning there was no answer. Her mother's premature death was an awful shock, but it was the gaping hole of that religious morning conversation that would haunt her most.

I never tired of Mum's company, whether it was folding the washing together, or watching her toil away in her garden or in mine. At the drop of a hat Mum was ready to make a cup of tea, cook a casserole, cuddle a screaming baby I couldn't settle or watch the children for half an hour so I didn't have to drag them all to the supermarket. Whilst she couldn't understand why I wanted to return to work part time after having each child, she supported me with practical help that made it possible: picking kids up, filling in for our nanny if she was sick or late. On the rare occasion when I was sick she assumed complete control: peas on my head, soup on the boil, there was never anything as nurturing or reassuring as having my mother take care of me. It was never time for her to go home. I liked having her around and, surprisingly, so did my husband. There must have been times when he would have rather she'd not been there, but having lost his own mother ten years before he was very clear: 'Mothers are sacred.'

If mothers are sacred, nanas are untouchable, the light in my children's day every day, for a few hours or just ten minutes. She was the only one who could love them as much as I did, if not more so because there was none of the frustration and the mundane to go with it.

Her role evolved with growing toddlers and she renewed her sewing skills that had lain dormant for thirty-five years because she was too busy with her own children.

Hours were spent buying loads of different material to make her granddaughters dresses, skirts, pyjamas and nightdresses.

Nana, their only living grandparent, was interested in every little thing they had to say, every dance they made up, every picture they wanted to draw for her, every noughts and crosses game, and any movie they wanted to watch. Sleepovers meant snuggling in Nana's bed with her, tea parties were allowed with the china cups that were off limits when I was little, and there were no limits on the desserts, with ice creams and whipped cream and anything else they could think of.

It wasn't that she had unlimited energy or no boundaries; she certainly knew when she'd had enough. I could see that one of the best parts of having grandchildren was being able to hand them back after a fun-filled day or in fact just a few hours of helping out with the ordinary.

Any time with Nana was special but there was something very special about 'treat day', a nominated afternoon where she would pick one of the kids up from kinder or school and spend a few hours alone with them having afternoon tea and shopping for material. Together they would mull over endless bright patterns, buttons and ribbons that would become a unique creation. Without fail each skirt or dress would draw attention, not only because of Mum's obvious flair for putting the unlikely together but because they would twirl. 'What's the use of a skirt that doesn't twirl when you spin around?' she would say to her granddaughters, and there was always a headband to match.

They loved it, but I felt like it made me look bad because I couldn't compete with the undivided attention and good fun. It was an uneven playing field where everyone was happy.

The time had come to tell the children, and the decision was made to be upfront; not warts and all but enough to put them in the picture of Nana not being well and what the medicines she had to take would do. It was explained without fanfare during an afternoon tea of cupcakes and chocolate milk in fancy cups. Like wide-eyed little puppies the heads of the three-, five- and six-year-old tilted sideways as their brains tried to understand what it all meant. Then came the questions.

'Is all your hair going to fall out?'

'Yes it is.'

'So will you be bald like Daddy?'

'Just like your daddy.'

'Will it grow back?'

'Probably. It might be spikey like a porcupine.'

Little hands clutched over their smiles at the thought of Nana looking like a porcupine as attention turned to ploughing through the last of the cupcakes. It appeared we had successfully navigated a minefield. Mum and I looked at each other with relief and I began to clear the table. It was in that unguarded moment that my considered six-year-old McKenzie spoke. 'Nana, are you going to die?'

I felt helplessly out of reach as I looked over at Mum still seated at the table with her granddaughters. She didn't return my gaze, which indicated she was going to handle the grenade.

'Well, you know, all living things must die one day, nothing and no one can live forever. The doctors are going to give me medicine to help me live longer, so hopefully that's something we don't have to worry about for a while.'

Not worry about for a while? I thought. The doctor said that few people get more than eighteen months. That's not a long time, it's the blink of an eye in my book. But to a six-year-old next week is a long way off. A year and a half was indeed 'a while'.

Nana's explanation seemed to be enough for McKenzie at that moment and the mood became lighter as Nana produced a box. 'Who wants to see my new hair?' There was an instant and loud chorus of 'Me', and they began to squabble over who was going to try the wig on first.

The inevitable began to happen within a few weeks of the treatment starting and, though Mum only mentioned in passing that clumps of hair had started to come away in her hand and brush, I knew the reality hurt more than she let on. Determined to take control she took herself off to the hairdresser and had the remaining hair shaved off, and the wig made its official debut. No one even noticed, which was exactly what she wanted. It wasn't that she was embarrassed at having a bald head, nor was it vanity, but a woman with a bald head 'screamed' cancer patient and frankly Mum wanted to keep it private and her life as normal as possible. It looked so good on her, almost better than her real hair: different shades of blonde in a chin-length multi-layered style that had a little bit of 'mess' to it so that it didn't look too perfect. It was a mask that could divert attention from the focus cancer commands, even if it was momentary.

I learnt to interpret the minor side effects of her treatment without having to repeatedly ask, 'What's wrong?' If she refused a cup of tea I knew it was because she had a metallic taste in her mouth and choosing soft foods meant her mouth was sore from ulcers.

When the bad days of chronic fatigue and nausea came they were somewhat eased by being in the comfort of her home, and true to form she made sure she was prepared. She didn't bother with smart outfits or her wig; instead she dressed her bedroom and transformed it into a warm cocoon. Natural light would stream through the sheer curtains, a small, pretty bunch of non-perfumed flowers would be placed on the dresser and her bed adorned with lots of big pillows, a fluffy dressing gown within reach. The bedside table was cluttered with everything that might be needed to ride out the bad day: a clock radio that was set to the same easy-listening station playing tunes that had filled my childhood, a lamp, a book and a crossword. Also jostling for space was the plethora of pills she needed to take, a large glass of water, sweets for her and the grandchildren and a lipstick, just in case we dropped in.

She wore Plumalicious

'The chemotherapy is doing its job,' said the oncologist. The first few rounds of chemotherapy were complete and Mum had done exactly as the doctor had recommended. We'd diligently complemented traditional medicine with nature's artillery and Mum deserved a good result. However, the doctor's neutral tone kept a lid on what might have been a reason to get excited. My gut told me there must be a caveat on the positive news.

The blood results revealed that the cancer tumour markers, the vital numbers that gauged whether the treatment was working to shrink the tumours, had dropped, but not significantly. I was disappointed that our dedicated effort hadn't shocked the cancer into remission and though I knew it would have been unlikely it didn't stop me wishing for it to happen. I wondered whether the small progress meant we could expect an extension on the eighteen-month timeline Mum had initially been given but I didn't ask the doctor. It was decided that the best course of action was to continue treatment with the drug she was on until it stopped having an effect.

We pressed on with our daily lives, which included uneventful routines and a gathering for the weekly family dinner.

A weekly family dinner was a permanent fixture in all our calendars. When we'd all begun to leave the family nest each child would visit Mum separately during any given week, but at least once during the course of seven days she would make sure we all came together for a home-cooked meal with generous side dishes of wine and sibling banter.

Mum had been a true homemaker. By her own admission all she'd ever wanted to do was be a stay-at-home mother, and after marrying Dad she'd closed her first florist shop to have children. A true mother hen but not in a storybook kind of way, she didn't help us with homework, or more likely didn't know how to, she never did tuckshop duty or baked cakes. In fact we used to joke about Mum's culinary repertoire, or lack of it. Most dinners were standard meat and three veg, Fridays was fish 'n' chips from the local shop and Mum's night off. 'What's for dessert?' was met with a lightning response: 'Apple, banana or orange.' It's not that Mum didn't love a dessert, she just didn't want to make them. The closest we used to get was a frozen apple, apricot or berry pie, and more often than not she would forget about it in the oven and burn 'the bum' of it. In most cases it would still be eaten, doused in cream and ice cream to hide the mishap. There was no disputing that she made fantastic spaghetti Bolognese (the secret was Worcestershire sauce), salmon patties, vegetable soup and an unbeatable roast.

Once a week Mum cooked a roast dinner; the crowd favourite was lamb. As children we would make a grab for the protruding bone that had very little meat but was crisp and salty; as adults nothing changed – a fight for the bone was a certainty. Accompaniments to the meat rarely changed: fresh shredded beans, peas with a pinch of sugar and crunchy roast potatoes. All the plates would be spread out along the kitchen bench and the meal dished according to who liked what.

The family dinner also became a 'sudden death' invitational for romance. When any of us brought a new love interest to the weekly gathering it indicated that a relationship might have longevity, but it could also mean the opposite. If the siblings gave the thumbs-down the invitee was in trouble; if our mother gave the thumbs-down it was all over.

'Never go somewhere empty-handed,' was her golden social rule, and it also applied to dinner with your family.

'I don't care if you walk in with a bottle of wine, a carton of milk, chocolates or a flower picked from a garden, it's the gesture,' Mum had drilled into all of us.

It was a cardinal sin if a guest at our family dinner walked in empty-handed. If it was combined with bad table manners or a failure to offer help, if they couldn't handle the loud playing field of our family, they were given the kiss of death. To be fair there were a few that would not have wanted to come back anyway, especially one young lady who found a strand of hair in her spaghetti. The lapse in hygiene control prompted cries of, 'Whose is that?', 'That's disgusting', 'It's long and blonde'. Seeing as I had cooked the dinner and my hair fitted the guilty profile, I claimed responsibility. 'Well at least you know it's a clean hair,' I laughed. Of course we all continued to eat the meal, except for the guest,

48

and moments after she left someone quipped, 'She ain't coming back!' and she didn't.

When our family home of twenty-five years was sold and Mum and my youngest brother Mick moved to a smaller place, the weekly dinner was hosted on rotation. After grandchildren began entering the mix, it made more sense to have it at the house best equipped to handle little ones, and that was usually mine. The weekly roast gave way to easier options of BBQs or casseroles and my sisters-in-law would lighten the load by bringing salads or dessert. Whatever the venue or the menu it was the same sequence: easy conversation, a few jibes, arguments over who cleaned up last time, girls doing more than the boys and a haphazard vote on whose wine was the pick of the night. No one was immune from a 'swipe' if they didn't bring something or pitch in.

'Where's your bottle of wine, you tight-arse?'

'Get off your backside and help clean up, you lazy prick.'

My older brother Robert had gone through a stage where the family dinner appeared to be just a duty call. He'd swan in, bring nothing, eat and leave soon after, but not before we all gave him a gobful.

'Oh, Robert's here, everyone. Hello, Robert, how nice of you to join us.'

'Would you like a drink, Rob? Which one did you bring again?'

'See ya later, Rob, thanks for popping in.'

The setting was permanently fixed at 'loud' or 'louder', but for all the ribbing and teasing and insults there was inbuilt radar that detected the need for restraint. Throughout the years if someone was nursing a broken heart, a bad business deal or just a tough time, a light but genuine family shield would surround them.

Family birthdays are just family dinners with the addition of a cake and candles. When we were growing up, Mum's lack of interest in baking meant that the six birthday cakes required each year were purchased from Patterson's cake shop. It was a standard order: chocolate sponge with big pieces of chocolate on top that we would all fight over.

Birthdays were just another thing Mum and I shared. I am July 7th, she July 6th, her best friend July 5th. As a child I never tired of Mum telling the story of how I interrupted her thirtieth birthday party. She claimed to have 'held on' until just after midnight so that I could have my own date on the calendar. There was a stage somewhere between the ages of eight and fifteen that I rued having to combine my family celebrations with hers, because I was counting down to my own birthday, but when that self-absorbed phase passed I found it to be another beautiful tie that bound us.

Mum had never been one to make a fuss of her own birthday, but we were both approaching milestones: her seventy and me forty. I certainly didn't want to mark mine with a big party, especially as I was well into my fourth pregnancy, but Mum was surprisingly open to a small celebration for her. It was highly unusual for her to agree to any sort of gathering that focused on her and I couldn't help but feel that she was using it as somewhat of an unofficial last supper. It seemed a strange irony that after ninety-four years in business Patterson's Cakes closed down a week before the lunch.

The guest list for Mum's gathering, apart from immediate family, was no more than ten. She wanted to keep it casual and was adamant that the grandchildren be included, which led to one obvious venue: my house.

An hour before everyone arrived I looked at the long table dressed with crisp white tablecloths and small vases of bright yellow daffodils down the middle. Daffodils, I thought. When did we become a daffodil type of family? My mother was a creator of exotic and magical floral centrepieces and the best I could come up with for her seventieth birthday was vases of daffodils. I frowned at the mismatch of different chairs that varied in height and colour. Mum and I had pooled our white crockery but it was still different, the wine glasses varied in shapes and stems and the overall look didn't seem fitting. It lacked polish, style or elegance, which annoyed me intensely. I chastised myself for not going all out and splurging on outsourcing the whole event to make it look like something from a magazine where everything looked effortlessly chic.

'That looks pretty,' Mum said when she arrived.

'It looks shit,' I scoffed. 'An absolute mosh pit.'

'Well the daffodils are lovely and bright,' she insisted.

'Yes, well, when the best bit you can think to pinpoint is the brightness of the cheap daffodils then I know it's shit.'

Mum laughed, I knew she agreed with me. 'What's it matter?' she said, grabbing the broom to finish off sweeping the floor. 'No one would notice but us anyway. Now go and finish your hair and put on a bright lipstick.'

As I applied my make-up I mentally ridiculed myself for being shallow, for worrying about mismatched chairs when my mother was dying and was about to celebrate what was possibly her last birthday. I chose the brightest red lipstick I could find and went back to the kitchen, where Mum was shoving the children's clutter into the laundry and out of sight, our standard 'make the house look clean' trick.

Once the first drink was poured and glasses 'clinked' the laughs began to flow as they invariably did, and my visions of a perfect setting gave way to the reality of red-wine spillages and funny stories shared among family and friends. Mum was surrounded by those she loved most; the gaggle of high-pitched grandchildren kept the mood light and their only pause was to see who could get closest to Nana when it was time to blow out the candles on her bright pink ice-cream cake in the shape of a Dolly Varden doll. It was a lovely day, mismatched decor and all.

The following morning warm cake and coffee with Mum and two of my oldest friends was a perfect start to my low-key birthday. Mum had known these girls since we were in early primary school together and had even done flowers for their weddings; she was extremely comfortable in their company and the feeling was mutual. Mum did away with her wig and we spent a few relaxing hours together as our young children played in the backyard.

After they'd left, Mum handed me my gift. I opened the box and under the mounds of tissue paper was a beautiful, gleaming Robur teapot. For Mum every day began and ended with a perfect pot of tea, never a teabag.

'It's just like yours,' I gushed.

'It *is* mine. I had the dents pulled out and the teapot polished for you.'

'But it was one of your wedding gifts. I don't want it. Why are you getting rid of all your stuff before you're gone?'

'I don't need a big pot anymore, I have a little one that's perfect, I want you to have it.'

I sighed heavily but knew arguing was pointless.

'It's beautiful. Thank you.'

'My pleasure. Now put your lipstick on and go to lunch, I can't be here all day.'

Another small group of girlfriends had insisted on acknowledging my milestone. Over a token glass of champagne at a little local restaurant, the gathering laughed at how a 'quick' lunch was far too civilised a way to celebrate turning forty. I decided there and then that the appropriate marking of my milestone would be delayed for exactly one year.

The thought of going out for dinner with my husband that night didn't appeal; the couch and early to bed seemed far more enticing. When I shared my thoughts with the gaggle of six women they gave their unsolicited opinions.

'Oh, don't be mean, he wants to do something nice.'

'It won't be a big night.'

'If he did nothing, he'd be accused of not making any effort.'

I laughed and conceded that Michael was in a no-win situation. Damned if he did and damned if he didn't. It was just that I was damn tired.

As soon as I returned home, Mum picked up her bag. 'OK, I'm off, I need to have a sleep. What are you wearing to dinner tonight?' she asked as she walked to the door.

'I only have one option that complements a thirty-week pregnant belly and swollen legs, the shimmering grey dress with the black swirl.'

'Yes, that dress is lovely. Make an effort, have your hair done, he is taking you somewhere nice,' she said.

'Where?' I groaned.

'I'm not telling,' she laughed, and off she went.

Have my hair done? A quick dinner does not require a special hairdo, I thought. I became suspicious. He wouldn't throw me a surprise party, would he? I'd be furious! That night as the car pulled up outside the city's tallest building I spotted a red carpet leading to the entrance. I kept my thoughts to myself but by that stage they were screaming: *He's organised a damn surprise party!*

As we stepped into the lift and it travelled skywards to the top level I remembered that there was a new restaurant boasting spectacular panoramic views of the city and my internal rant calmed down. Oh good, it *is* just dinner, I thought, and relief washed over me as I stepped out of the lift and looked right. There was nothing! Then I looked left: 'Surprise!'

Sixty friends and family had gathered for the birthday I didn't want to celebrate for another year. My mother and the girls I had spent the morning and lunch with had all been in on it and knew I would have caught on if they'd ditched our plans to catch up.

Mum looked radiant in her pale blue dress and I twigged that her claim earlier in the day that she needed to go home and sleep was so that she would be able to enjoy the night. As I leant in to kiss her she whispered sarcastically, 'I knew you'd be thrilled, now don't forget to smile.' Photos and more photos. 'Smile.' Click.

It was easy to have a nice time surrounded by those I loved, most of whom enjoyed ribbing me about drinking water whilst they drank champagne. 'We're loving your birthday,' they chortled throughout the night. I moved around the room having the same conversation as to whether I'd suspected my Michael's covert plans, and repeatedly agreed that the setting that showcased Melbourne's city lights was indeed amazing.

Mum was also making her way through the room speaking to everyone. She knew almost all of them and had for a long time; she had always loved my friends. It was better than being the guest of honour, fun without too much focus.

Michael made a short speech and toast, to which I had no choice but to say a totally unprepared 'Thank you' to everyone. There, front and centre, was my mother and without thinking I blurted out my gratitude to her. 'Thank you, Mum, for fighting so hard to stay with us.' Many in the room knew our world had been shattered over the past eight weeks but some didn't. Looking at her that night it was still hard to believe: the matriarch dressed as elegantly as ever, with the best wig ever, beautiful make-up and a grin from ear to ear.

As we drove home that night Michael was keen to tell me how he had pulled the night together and how hard it had been to get a comprehensive list of guests given that I had different groups of friends. 'I think I may have forgotten a few,' he said.

'Ah yes, you did, that's going to be awkward.'

I couldn't help but ask what possessed him to throw a party, especially when he knew I wanted to wait until the following year.

'Yes, your mother said you wouldn't be happy.'

I was mildly annoyed at him for ignoring my mother's advice when usually he was smart enough to follow it.

'So why spend a ridiculous amount of money on a night you knew I didn't want?'

His reply was gentle. 'Because I didn't want to wait until next year.'

It was then I realised that in fact my birthday celebration wasn't actually about me at all.

She wore Mulberry

D o you think you're the sacrificial lamb?' I asked Mum
as we sat in my sun-drenched family room watching
the children on the swings outside.

'Yes, I wondered that. I certainly prayed that I would
be taken instead of the baby,' she admitted.

Two months before Mum's diagnosis our family had
been rocked by another discovery. I'd been blasé about
the standard twenty-week scan of my fourth child until
it revealed a growth in one lung, which in a worst-case
scenario threatened to suffocate the baby in utero. Our
emotional pendulum swung between 'it will be all right'
and imagining how one would prepare the death notice. The
latter seemed achingly close as we entered our third week
of scans and watched helplessly as the growth enlarged to
push the baby's heart over to the wrong side of its tiny body.

I prayed with a vigilance not practised since my Catholic primary school years. I visualised pink bubbles that contained images of my healthy baby and sent them off into the universe and on my way to scans repeated affirmative mantras of the future: 'Our baby was born healthy in September 2009.'

I mentally brokered deals with God, the devil, my dead father and anyone else I could think of for the health of our unborn child. I carried angels, lucky charms and gratefully accepted the prayers of others. One friend's grandmother, whom I had never met, offered the pressure cooker variety: intense praying practised several times a day. We welcomed everything. Through it all, day in day out, was my mother, helping to keep the house and family going, acting as a human shield when I needed it, babysitting, cooking, listening and just being. Little did I know she was also offering herself in exchange for the safety of her grandchild.

At week twenty-six came the turning point, as was typical with the condition. The baby began outgrowing the lesion and the proverbial light at the end of the tunnel peeked through. As the weekly scans continued, cautious optimism entered our lives again. They say all things are relative but how quickly we forgot the flipside, the sliding-doors scenario.

As the due date drew near it looked probable that our fourth child would enter the world with minimal fuss. We were lucky but there was also a bittersweet feeling that Mum's secret deal with the devil had been called in.

On the 16th September, my husband and I went out for a quick dinner around the corner from home to celebrate his birthday. The 'bump' was already two days overdue but during the meal I felt a shift and casually announced:

'The baby will come tomorrow.'

'OK, and you know this because?'

'Because I know, mark my words.'

Around six am the next morning I felt the twinge of a contraction.

As a mother of more than one knows, there is not much time for anything within the first few weeks of having of a newborn other than feeding, changing nappies and washing. It was the last chance I had to complete my 'to do' list, and that required a trip to our local large shopping mall. Mum was my designated driver because I knew full well that at some stage she'd be driving me to the hospital, my bag packed with clothes for the baby, and me in the back of the car. It took almost four hours to complete the list. We stopped every

now and then for the odd contraction but there was no
need to panic; they still weren't worth timing. During
the process of exchanging Michael's birthday shirts I
paused for a sharp pain that caught me a little off guard.
The assistant looked concerned. 'Are you OK?'

'Oh yes. I'm just in the early stages of labour.'

Mum and I had started to giggle but the shop
assistant didn't seem to share the joke and the transaction
was completed quickly, perhaps in an effort to make
sure I didn't give birth on the shop floor.

'Do you think we should go to the hospital now?'
Mum asked.

'Soon,' I said. 'But let's have something to eat before
we go.'

'First bub?' enquired the waiter as he handed us the
menus. I laughed at the suggestion. 'No, fourth!'

'Wow. When are you due?'

'Yesterday,' Mum said, laughing

'Really? When do you think it will come?'

'Later today.'

'How do you know that? Mother's intuition?'
he joked.

'No, because the contractions are starting to ramp
up now.'

The food arrived promptly.

Once in the car the pains that had been coming a little closer together disappeared. 'Let's drop in at your house for a cup of tea,' I suggested.

Mum disagreed. 'I think we should just go straight to the hospital. It's starting to rain and the traffic will be slow.'

'Come on!' I pleaded. 'It will be the last decent cup I get for a few days. Please.'

She capitulated and steered the car towards her house. As we entered the driveway a killer contraction gripped my lower abdomen.

'On second thoughts, let's go to the hospital.'

My mother said nothing but gave me a 'Mother knows best!' look.

I called Michael and my obstetrician. It was showtime!

It was never the plan for Mum to be present at any of my children's births; she knew the right measure of involvement and when to step back. Given that the sand in the hourglass was obviously running out, though, I had asked her a few weeks beforehand if she'd like to be in the delivery room. She was very touched at the gesture but maintained her position 'That time is for a husband and wife.' As the contractions increased there was still no sight of my husband or obstetrician but there was Mum right by my side.

I politely but firmly asked the nurse to find the anaesthetist to deliver the pain relief; I wasn't intimating Panadol, I was thinking of an epidural. Seconds later Professor Sue entered the room, not the anaesthetist but the specialist who had scanned my problematic bump since week twenty. 'Your doctor is stuck in traffic so he rang me and asked if I would help out until he arrives.'

I'm sure it's quite common for many women to have an irrational attachment to their obstetrician. I had complete trust in the man who had delivered our other three children safely into the world. I'd teased him several times that we operated on a 'cash on delivery' basis and that if he missed it there would be no payment; I'd never considered that he wouldn't actually make it to the delivery in time — surely I was his favourite?

Even through the increasing pain I could see the irony of the situation: the two men I needed most were nowhere within reach, but the most important women were. However, I failed to see the irony in what Professor Sue said next. 'Oh, and there will be no anaesthetist.'

'WHAT? Are you kidding me?'

'No I'm not kidding — it's time. Push!'

Enter husband, exit baby.

With all the latest equipment on standby we waited to hear and see whether the growth in the baby's lungs would have any effect on its first few breaths. It didn't! The sounds of a newborn cry filled the room.

It all happened quickly and everyone was so focused on the wellbeing of the baby that there was no mention of whether it was a boy or a girl: the perfectly wrapped bundle was simply placed on my chest.

'What flavour is it?' I asked

Without saying a word, Professor Sue pulled back the towel.

'Is that what I think it is? It's a boy?'

Our boy's name had been decided some six years ago but we had never required it. James Tosca, Tosca being my father's nickname.

After three girls, all of a sudden we had a son. Who would've thought? My mother was bursting with happiness until we exchanged one of 'those' looks through misty eyes. It was a priceless, unplanned golden moment. Our bond couldn't get any closer. Her baby giving birth to her own baby, one she wouldn't get to see grow up. Cue tears, photos and the arrival of my obstetrician.

She wore Love That Pink

Once Mum began having chemotherapy it became obvious that eventually she would need my help more than I would need hers.

The desire to live close to my mother was nothing new. As soon as I became pregnant with my first child we sold our bayside home to move to an area dubbed by many 'nappy valley'. It was a move back to my roots but more importantly it placed me a stone's throw from where Mum lived. Being walking distance from each other was the difference between seeing her once a day and many times.

After a few years Mum moved to a new house. It was only a 10-minute drive away but it wasn't the same and I was forever looking for places that would bring her closer again. The search was originally and largely for my benefit; a renewed and more pressing search was for Mum's.

On a cold August morning my husband for no reason at all had taken a detour in his daily walk with the dog and noticed a 'for lease' sign at the end of our street. 'Fate,' we mused and I picked up the phone straightaway. It was answered immediately

'Good morning.'

'Found you a house.'

'Where?'

'Michael saw it this morning, it's at the end of our street.'

'Darling the rent will be too expensive. A slaughter of money!'

'I don't care, we will pay the rent.'

'I don't want you to pay the rent, I can pay my own rent. I'm fine where I am.'

'Tick-tock, Mum, your clock is running out. I want to organise to at least look at it.'

A day later my brother Steve was standing with Mum in the empty townhouse and within minutes knew it was ideal. It ticked all the boxes: natural light and a bright kitchen. There were two lovely rooms with big floor-to-ceiling windows, one for her to sew in, and the other, which had a small ensuite, would be her bedroom. A cosy lounge room opened onto a courtyard and garden, or what could become one, and it had a huge lock-up garage with an automatic door that provided her with security when arriving home at night. The only negative was the pink-peach-coloured walls.

Mum rang me at work after the inspection and I could hear excitement in her voice.

'It's lovely, it's perfect. I can learn to love pink walls.'

'It's meant to be!' I declared. 'It has your name written all over it. I haven't seen it up for lease in the six years we have lived in the street – did the estate agent say what happened to the last tenant?'

'Yes, it was an elderly man, he died.'

'What, in the house?'

'Yes.'

'Oh, does that bother you?'

'No, don't be ridiculous. It's my turn next.'

'Good one, Mum.'

'Well it's true!' She laughed.

That night Steve rang and said he had spoken to the estate agent.

'I've told the agent that we will paint the place at our own expense. It's fine the way it is, but a coat of white paint will freshen it up and make it perfect.'

The lease was signed within days, and a few weeks later Mum was on the move. She was a mere fifty metres away from me, only two hundred metres from Steve, Vink and their two children, and around five hundred metres from Mick and his wife Haillie.

As soon as the boxes were unpacked Mum set to work in the garden that had been neglected. In every house she had lived, whether it was rented or owned, Mum had put enormous effort into creating a beautiful garden. As a kid I had watched her spend entire Saturday afternoons planting perennials, leaving a trail of little black plastic pots behind her. She derived so much pleasure from the process and found endless enjoyment seeing the bursts of colour. Her new home was no different and she transformed it into a happy and peaceful oasis.

Sleepovers at Nana's resumed for my little girls, and they were so excited to walk down to her house alone. I would farewell them at our front gate with their overnight bags and was able to see Mum at the other end of the street also supervising the unaccompanied journey.

The move provided greater spontaneity, lots of bite-sized simple but lovely experiences. It was dropping in for afternoon tea almost every day as we walked home from school; Mum could walk up to have dinner when she felt like it even if it was at the last minute, or I could drop down dinner on a plate, no containers required. With a spare fifteen minutes I would drop in for a cup of tea or with a spare five minutes I could leave the car running, drop in to say hi, give her a kiss, see if she needed anything and walk out again. Almost every morning on our way to school Nana would be standing out on the front porch waving as we walked past her, the kids singing in chorus from across the road.

'Good moooorning, Nana.'

Even her next-door neighbour started opening his door to exchange morning greetings with the tribe.

I could check on Mum without overdoing it by reading simple key signals. Her bedroom window could be seen from the street. If the curtains were closed I knew she was resting; if the hall light could be seen from the street I knew she was home.

Home had always been her sanctuary and within just a few weeks it looked like she had been living there for years. It didn't matter to her that she didn't own it. There was no surprise when she announced that this home was where she wanted to die.

As the pages of the calendar turned towards December we began to plan our family Christmas Day lunch, just as we had done every year.

A new venue was the only change to our festive-season proceedings. Steve and his wife Vink had just finished renovating their home and it was decided that upon completion they would host. With a new baby I was delighted to have the reprieve and better still it was walking distance.

In late November at one of our weekly dinners we organised the family Kris Kringle, which included siblings, sisters-in-law and Mum. The gift-buying allocation produced a predictable script:

'I think we should make it two hundred dollars each this year.'

'No way, a hundred dollars tops, I don't want two hundred dollars worth of crap.'

'If I get Michael Curtain he's getting cash or a voucher, he returns what he gets anyway.'

The names were then drawn from a bowl, though it was standard for everyone to secretly swap the names later in an effort to make their gift buying easier.

The Christmas tree in my house post a few hours of decorating looked nothing like those in shop windows, and more like a dog's breakfast. The higher branches looked decidedly sparse whereas the lower sprigs were weighed down heavily with ornaments where small hands had been able to reach. When the children were born

Mum had given each of the kids a personalised bauble, and they would rummage through all the decorations just to find the one with their name on it and hang it front and centre. I had to resist the urge to rearrange the uneven distribution at least until after they had gone to bed.

When the tree was complete the final decoration was the garland for the front door. A few years earlier Mum had created a beautiful ring of clear beads with silver stars for each of her children's households. They were all slightly different but unmistakably her handiwork. Once it adorned the entrance to our home, it really began to feel like Christmas.

Mum was enjoying many of the season's activities: attending McKenzie's end-of-year concert and Sidney's preschool nativity play. She would make trips to her old flower wholesaler and fill her children's homes with pots of bright red poinsettias and glorious white Christmas lilies that would be in full bloom for December 25th.

Mum was organised, and had finished making James's Santa sack, which was a variation of the sacks she had made for her other six grandchildren. It was a far cry from the printed pillowcases we'd had as kids and four times the size. I joked that with her generous proportions it would cost Father Christmas a bloody fortune to fill the damn thing. Each one had different Christmas trinkets attached to them; some had bells, others had angels or stars and the child's name embroidered in bright red letters. They were all unique, but all of them had a little label inside that read: 'Made with love from Nana.'

The odds suggested it would be Mum's last Christmas, and even if it wasn't chances were that in another twelve months her condition would leave little to be merry about. In spite of what was looming, no symbolic changes were made to mark Mum's last Christmas and that's just the way she wanted it. And in a bizarre chain of events it was our dog that took centre stage and diverted our attention.

Our canine Lili was a cottonball-coloured golden retriever. She had been Michael's and my wedding present to each other a decade beforehand. The volumes of hair that she continuously shed drove us mad but she was a glorious animal inside and out. She had happily shared her domain whenever a new child entered the fold, and was an excellent guard dog and a lovely walking companion, unless she smelled food: then she was a runaway train.

Months before Mum's cancer was diagnosed Lili had been staying very close to her whenever she would visit. Whenever Mum sat down the dog moved to rest her head on Mum's lap or feet, and she'd receive a loving pat and a few words

'What's up with you, Lili dog? What do you want?'

Lili would tilt her head into Mum's hand, look at her as if she was talking with her big brown eyes and then lie down again. We would later wonder whether Lili, with her breed's renowned sense of smell, knew something way before we did.

Just after James was born Lili had begun to limp, and every now and then both her back legs would give way under her. We promptly made an appointment with the local vet and whinged about the prospect of having to pay for an expensive hip replacement, only to be devastated when an X-ray revealed that she was riddled with cancer.

We sought advice but the treatment available was limited and wouldn't save her. We were willing to proceed with treatment as long as it didn't involve undue pain and allowed a comfortable existence but questioned whether it was kinder to euthanise her. We desperately wanted to do the right thing by this beautiful, loyal beast and were assured that we would know the right time to have her put down.

Early on Christmas Eve Lili could barely summon the energy to lift her head and her breathing was laboured. By lunchtime she had rallied so we put her on the lead, grabbed the kids and walked up to the clinic to have her checked out. Michael met us in the car.

Within a few minutes we were advised to take her to another vet with better facilities. It was too far for us to walk. 'I'll take the dog and you walk the kids home,' Michael suggested.

I started to pile the kids out onto the street as Michael lifted the dog into the back seat and shut the door.

'It's Christmas Eve, don't let the dog die on Christmas Eve,' I whispered to him.

Michael joined us at the neighbourhood Christmas drinks before the carol service.

'Where is the dog?' I asked

'At the clinic. They are giving her pure oxygen to help her.'

'What?'

'You said not to let the dog die on Christmas Eve, so that's what we need to do. She might need to be there for a couple of days.'

As we filled the children's stockings that night, the empty spot in the hallway where Lili would watch over the household felt like the Grand Canyon. The silent night held no magic as Michael and I lay in bed. We knew that the end was close for Lili and that the tough decision would have to be made soon.

Squeals of excitement filled the house in the pre-dawn as the children discovered what Santa had left, but for Michael and me the light and joyous mood was soon shattered by a call from the vet.

'Please come quickly. Lili has taken a turn for the worse and the oxygen is no longer working.'

I immediately rang Mum and asked her to come and sit with the children, who were so entranced with their gifts that our departure barely registered.

There was no decision for us to make when we arrived at the veterinary clinic – fate had already stepped in. 'I'm afraid we're going to have to put Lili down,' the vet said. We were then told what to expect. 'It won't hurt, there will be no pain and it will be very quick.'

Our loyal companion of ten years was lying on a soft blanket on the floor of the sterile room; her breathing was laboured and we sat down on the floor next to her. We were left alone with Lili to say goodbye and Michael and I openly cried as we stroked her thick white coat and spoke softly to her about having been such a good dog. 'She knows,' I said.

The vet came back into the room and we cradled Lili in our arms. Within five seconds of the lethal fluid being administered her eyes closed and she was gone.

I was shocked at the quiet and instant process of her death. In some ways I was glad there was no suffering or signs of pain or distress, but it was almost too quick. We were drained and broken and it was only nine am on Christmas morning.

We hadn't told the kids where we were going and they were so excited to show Nana their Christmas gifts that they didn't ask. Nor did they ask when we returned, so we said nothing and decided we would only tell them when they asked.

Christmas Day rolled on with the predictable light arguments over who was going to peel the prawns and ten experts giving advice on the cooking of the turkey on the BBQ. Despite so many 'chiefs' in the kitchen no one ever seemed to remember to add water to the pot boiling the prized Christmas pudding.

As the children played, the adults sat down at the long table that Mum had beautifully decorated with centrepieces of fresh holly and Christmas berries. We raised our glasses 'to Lili'.

No one even dared to think of what next Christmas would be like.

She wore Amethyst Smoke

The New Year had been rung in at a family friend's wedding and Mum glowed in the happy snaps of her surrounded by her children and in-laws. A week later we were in a meeting with palliative care.

It seemed a premature appointment to have, especially when the treatment looked to be holding the status quo. On paper Mum's medical condition wasn't improving but it certainly wasn't going downhill. She looked well and her hair had grown back into a short chic silver-grey cropped style that she liked. Some days she preferred the security of the wig, and I don't know why but she chose to wear it when the nurse from palliative care came to visit. We sat at her kitchen table with the male nurse, enjoying a cup of tea. Mum was as bright as a button; it was as if the talk we were about to have about dying was for someone else.

'We are going to do everything we can to support you when you reach the palliative stage and it should be relatively easy for your loved ones to care for you in your home, Pamela.'

He talked us through how the home visits worked and all the support structures available to help us achieve her wish to die in peace and privacy, but his words of experience also offered caution. 'Sometimes, despite the best-laid plans, in the end a hospice is the best choice for everyone.'

Mum and I smiled at each other knowingly. Not us, was what we were both smugly thinking.

There are many reasons people might choose not to die at home, especially a family home in which loved ones need to keep living. Mum's new home was merely on loan; it was the perfect place for her to die.

The meeting ended with no immediate plans to schedule another visit. It was open ended and again we were assured that assistance would be available whenever we wanted it.

'Well I don't think we'll be needing him for a while,' I said confidently to Mum as we closed the front door.

It's not that we were running from the inevitable – or maybe we were. Mum looked healthy and for the most part felt good; we simply hadn't considered that her body had put up a smokescreen to conceal what was really going on. The next blood results showed a rise in the dreaded cancer markers, those crucial numbers that indicate the growing or shrinking of a tumour. They were moving in the wrong direction.

'There are no other options to try,' the doctor said.

I desperately tried to recall what at our first meeting seemed like a long list of available chemotherapy drugs but could think of nothing. I immediately offered Mum up as a guinea pig to try any experimental drugs, or trials but was told there were none she would be eligible for. Everything else that may have been discussed in the minutes that followed found no place in my memory because my mind charged forward to where I might find somewhere there *would* be other options.

In the back of my mind I was conscious of the agreement I had made with Mum, even though I had no intention of honouring it. I was hoping that she wasn't going to announce that she had held up her end of the bargain to try treatment and that she wanted me to fulfil my part and let her stop.

Nothing of any relevance was discussed until we were back in the car.

'Well, I guess that's the end of that then,' Mum said with resignation and a poker face.

'I don't think so!' I said adamantly. 'I really like the doctor and I know she is highly recommended but I want to investigate other alternatives and see if anyone else has something that maybe you can try.'

I was waiting for my mother to tell me to 'stop being a bull at a gate', to say 'it is what it is', or indeed to remind me of our agreement, but she didn't. In fact, her response took me quite by surprise. 'You know there was a doctor when I was having my chemo treatment twenty years ago that was into different therapies. I'm sure I've got her name written down somewhere.'

It was the green light. My mother, the same woman who a few months before had been adamant she wouldn't have treatment, was giving me the go-ahead to keep fighting for her. With a mixture of relief and renewed vigour I couldn't resist giving her a gentle ribbing. 'Well, haven't you changed your tune!'

Maybe her determination was sparked by the announcement that there was another grandchild on the way. My big brother Robert's second child was due in September. Whatever the reason I didn't need encouragement, and I extended my research to find anything that would give us hope. I knew we were likely to be grasping at straws but I wasn't ready to throw in the towel; more importantly, neither was Mum.

I had heard about the benefits of pine needles and bought packets of drugs derived from them. I tracked down the doctor Mum had spoken of and she put me in touch with another doctor who knew someone who knew someone, and a week later we arrived in the waiting room of Dr John.

We sat across from the small-statured man summarising the treatment of the past eight months, eager to hear his recommendations. He didn't offer a cure or even a gauge of how much extra time we could expect but he was willing to try a new combination of drugs, and we were willing to try anything.

'Well I won't die wondering, will I?' Mum said, smiling, as she grasped my hand.

I felt somewhat treacherous as I wrote a note of thanks and farewell to the oncologist that we had been seeing for eight months. Our gratitude was genuine and we'd grown very fond of her and the amazing support team but we didn't have time for loyalty and had nothing to lose by trying alternatives.

Being under new medical management didn't change the familiar process of Mum's treatment – only the location was different. We were still captive to tumour marker number counts and held our breath each time the doctor would deliver the latest result. I knew Mum missed the friendly banter of the ladies she had got to know – the new hospital was missing the patient camaraderie – but we knew we had to look past that and keep our eye on the prize of a longer life. Nevertheless, I did feel a little sad when I would drop her off for treatment, even if it was only for a few hours. 'Don't be ridiculous. I've got my book. I'm fine!' she'd insist.

I continued scouring the Internet looking for anything and anyone anywhere in the world that might strengthen our position in the battle but knew Mum was not an exceptional case or even good guinea-pig material. She was seventy years old with asthma, eczema and advanced breast cancer; even I knew there were no compassionate grounds for medical consideration. Her case was sad but not tragic, except for us.

I contacted the Chinese herbalist I had seen during my pregnancies to help the poor circulation in my legs and he made a concoction for Mum to help the inflammation of her liver. I knew firsthand how bad they tasted and that I was pushing the limits when I instructed Mum to drink the cocktail two or three times a day.

'I'm not drinking those anymore, they're disgusting,' she said after a week or two. I knew better than to argue a lost cause.

Despite being buoyed every time I read a survivor story where diet was credited as the cure, logic would place a small handbrake on my enthusiasm. I had never known Mum to be anything but a clean eater – a very clean eater: raw salads of tomatoes and onions were on her plate every day and had been for as far as my memory would reach. The same foods that were now being hailed as heavy hitters in the fight against cancer hadn't prevented her cancer twenty years ago. Maybe they had helped her recover from it, but if they had then why had it returned?

'Stress causes cancer,' was Mum's opinion.

'What have you got to be stressed about?' was my retort.

'Remember when I was hit by that car reversing in a car park? My legs were caught in between two cars. A year later I was diagnosed with cancer.'

I started to laugh in a mocking tone. 'Is that right, Dr Curtain? You've got to be kidding.'

'No, I'm convinced that triggered it.'

'All right, and what do you attribute the return of the cancer to?'

'I don't know, old age? She laughed. 'Doesn't matter now anyway, does it?'

No it didn't. The end was coming no matter how many spices or tomatoes she consumed, all I was hoping for was a little more time. Deep down though I knew that regardless of any time we were granted I would always want 'just a little more time'.

Without invitation 'Cancer' had become another member of our family, the one no one liked but was forced to accommodate. The initial shock of Mum's diagnosis had rocked all of us but the world didn't stop. One day I was shocked to find her scrubbing her bathroom.

'What are you doing, Mum?'

'What does it look like I'm doing?'

'For God's sake, you shouldn't be doing that.'

'Why not, you fool? Did you expect to find me curled up in a ball? I like a clean bathroom.' She was laughing at me. 'We have to get on with it.'

She was right! Cancer and the devastation that it promised to bring us didn't mean school lunches were no longer needed or that dinners weren't required. Children still woke up early and washing needed to be done.

We had to keep living, there would continue to be a family dinner each week, she still put in her Lotto numbers, the same ones she had taken for thirty-odd years. Cancer just meant that we now also had to allocate time for appointments, blood tests and chemotherapy. It simply had to fit in with the routine and mundane.

As the weeks went by, the only time cancer commanded and was permitted centre stage in our lives was on the day we would receive test results.

Sitting in the doctor's room, Mum would say something philosophical.

'What will be will be.'

'Yeah, thanks, Mum. You know what you can do with your cliché, don't you?'

For a few months, under the guidance of Dr John, nothing seemed to change much for better or worse and the tumour marker numbers remained steady. Mum still continued to look quite healthy though fatigue had increased its creep on her, but she adapted by making time for a nap each day. A 'bad' day was par for the course and didn't trigger alarm bells. She knew the way forward was to surrender to her body's signals and go to bed.

As summer became autumn there were still many good days and occasions to enjoy. I would find her at the sewing machine surrounded by bags of different fabrics, boxes of bright beads and ribbons. There was a never-ending longing for more twirling skirts, pyjamas or bags for the kids' library books. Mum wasn't interested in making complicated pieces, although in her youth her skills had produced debutante gowns and bridesmaid dresses for friends. In the past twelve months she had even sewn a few simple summer dresses for me; until then the number of creations she had ever made me was a grand total of two.

I was seven when I went shopping with her for the white material that would become my First Communion dress. With excitement I watched her at the big round white kitchen table as she cut out the pattern and ignored my plea to make it floor length.

'It's your First Communion not your wedding,' she'd said.

As she placed the material under the needle of the old Singer sewing machine and her foot on the floor pedal, she stuck out her bottom lip in concentration and then the sewing commenced. I loved my dress and the short veil she made that had ribbons and artificial flowers either side. The creation was a fabulous success, though the same couldn't be said for the other creation, which was for my final school year formal.

We had seen a stunning brocaded gown with wide puffed sleeves and a dropped waist on the front cover of a glossy magazine; the price was almost a thousand dollars.

'You know I think I could make that,' Mum declared.

A search for fabric similar to the picture failed and somehow we ended up choosing a metallic electric-blue material with a black felt pattern on it.

I watched Mum's bottom lip poke out and over as she sat at the sewing machine, focused on creating the designer copy – a task that was clearly a lot harder than she'd thought, but she wouldn't let it beat her.

The photo album shows me smiling in my bespoke gown that didn't really resemble the glossy cover original, and I recall that the wide half-moon sleeves Mum had put wire in to make them stand out were bent by the end of the night. With the passing years that dress had stood the test of time as a butt of jokes on fashion faux pas.

'Yup, that was a shocker,' Mum would say, and shake her head whenever we came across the photo. Perhaps the dresses she had made me over the last twelve months were her redemption from sewing failure.

'Can you teach me to sew?' I asked as I watched her one afternoon.

'I didn't think you were very interested and you're so busy with the kids. I never had time to sew when you were little.'

'Well, I'm not really interested to be honest …'

'Thanks very much.' She laughed.

'… but I'm worried that if I don't learn to sew now it will be too late when you die, and then who will do the Santa sacks?'

Over the next few weeks I'd put baby James to sleep in the portable cot in her room and we would make tea and hunker down in the sewing room for a few hours to make her trademark Santa sacks, the master watching over her apprentice.

Mum was still getting out and about. She was always at local markets looking for interesting finds and could never resist specials on fresh produce even if she had no use for them. 'Going broke saving money,' she would say mockingly and hand me a huge box of tomatoes or bags of fruit.

The pregnancy of the pending grandchild reached the halfway mark and my brother and sister-in-law announced at the weekly family dinner that at the twenty-week scan they were going to find out the baby's sex. 'Really?' the siblings chimed.

There were seven grandchildren to date and we had all waited for the birth to find out what 'flavour' the baby was. 'And Nana is going to come with us,' said Robert.

That's not like Mum, I thought. Why would she go? I looked at Mum with eyebrows raised.

I saved my thoughts for when we were alone.

'They asked me to come,' she said before I had even asked the question.

'I've asked you before and you said no. You said that it was for a husband and wife, not a mother-in-law.'

'I know,' she said, not offering any further explanation.

'The baby is due in September, Mum, it's already April. You're not planning on being here in September? What aren't you telling me?'

'Nothing! On my dying word of honour, there is nothing you don't know, you know more than I do.'

The scan revealed a growing healthy baby boy and at the same time Rob and Sharon decided to name him. Rob rang each of the siblings to relay the double announcement.

'It's a boy and we're naming him Bentley.'

Our reactions were all similar: 'Oh, another boy, that's great. You're calling him what?'

The first wine at the next family dinner was a toast to the health of the baby that wouldn't enter the world for another five months; the second wine had only just been poured when the collective started pouring scorn on the choice of name.

'You can't call your son Bentley, you just can't.'

'Why not?'

'You've already got a son called Harley. You're not a car dealer, you idiot.'

'Fuck off.'

More wine, more wisecracks, more car-name suggestions filled the evening, and all the while Mum smiled and laughed here and there but said nothing.

What I didn't know at the time was what Mum had already confided in my brother Robert outside the hospital that day. 'I'm not going to make it!'

He had refused to enter into a debate. 'Of course you will.'

'I'm not going to make it!' she repeated.

Another Mother's Day came around and our family gathered to celebrate all the mothers in our growing clan. It had been a year since cancer had demanded a place in our lives but it had no place at our table, where the standard menu was casual food, lots of wine and family ribbing.

The trees were losing their final leaves before winter and Mum enjoyed long lazy weekends with a girlfriend who lived in the country with a beautiful garden that Mum had spent countless hours helping create. They planted roses, snowdrops, daffodils and Mum's favourite flower of all, gardenias. The gardenia bushes produced majestic white flowers almost the size of a small plate; the secret was to add Vegemite to the water. The two friends would tend to the blooms and shrubs then sit and enjoy sunny afternoons there before retiring by a log fire at night.

Sitting with a cup of tea one afternoon after her return I listened to tales of her relaxing few days and I felt a wave of envy.

'We should go on a holiday together. Just you and me.'

'That sounds nice – where would we go?'

'How about a health retreat?'

'No thanks, I don't want to get up at dawn and eat celery sticks.'

'Me neither. They won't let you have wine either.'

A few moments later I revisited the idea. 'It could be really good for you though, just to relax and have massages and good food. You're not drinking anyway and I guess I could go without wine for two or three days.'

'I don't mind where we go as long as we're together. You book somewhere, my shout.'

'I'll pay, Mum.'

'Just let me do this for us, let me do it while I can.'

Within a few days I had booked us on a three-day retreat to escape the winter, departing August 13th for the Queensland hinterland. It would be only the second time we had gone away together alone – the first had been ten years earlier. We began counting down the days.

In the blink of an eye July arrived and we were once again celebrating our birthdays. Mum had made it through another year – one that according to medical predictions she wouldn't have seen had she not received treatment. It was a hard thought to grasp, though I didn't dwell on it. My mother was stronger than statistics, I assured myself. If we were hanging our hat on numbers then in theory Mum would only have four months left. The first oncologist had said that even with treatment not many patients survive more than eighteen months. From where I was standing it looked certain that Mum would defy the odds. She looked good, had good quality of life and that was our benchmark: quality of life. Perhaps that alone was a reason to mark our birthdays with a party, but Mum actually never really liked parties and it was agreed that we would do nothing more than the weekly family dinner.

'Let's go out,' suggested my youngest brother Mick, who had no children.

'No, too hard with kids, it's stressful,' I protested.

'All right, well leave the kids at home and let's go Mexican, Taco Bill's.'

'Are you kidding,' I scoffed. 'Can we do a little better than that?'

'Don't be such a snob. It's close, and we can eat early. It's quick and Mum likes the margaritas.'

I looked to Mum for support in killing off the idea but she shrugged her shoulders. 'Who cares? It's close.'

On the morning of Mum's birthday I took her shopping for the winter coat she wanted; it was my gift to her. We had been in the shop no more than ten minutes when she made her choice. She was a savvy and impulsive shopper, whereas I 'um' and 'ah' fifty times before making a decision.

'I like this one,' she said, holding up the big long black puffy jacket.

She tried on two sizes before choosing the bigger.

'You can certainly wear either,' was my opinion. 'But I think the smaller one fits you a little better.'

Ignoring my opinion she headed to the counter with the bigger size. As we waited for the payment to be processed I suddenly realised my mother's motive.

'You're getting the bigger size so I can wear it when you're gone, aren't you?' Nothing was said, she just gave me a 'look'. I knew that look and knew not to argue.

I dropped her home so that she could rest ahead of our big night out at Taco Bill's. 'Bring the kids around after school for afternoon tea,' she suggested. 'I don't want them to miss out on blowing out candles.'

After I collected the children from school we dropped into Nana's, where she had prepared a tea party complete with princess crowns and other sparkly birthday essentials. Mum's sister Mary-Ann was there and we lit and relit the candles until everyone had a turn at blowing them out.

That night as I sat with Mum, siblings and sisters-in-law around a wooden table with café chairs, I shared my mock disgust at the standard of celebrations. 'This is not how I had envisaged my forty-first birthday.' The effort made was zero, not even a birthday cake. The waiter came out with two sombreros that Mum and I were asked to put on as we were presented with two pieces of sticky date pudding with sparklers on. All that was left to do was sing 'Happy Birthday' and laugh at the absurdity.

'Smile darling,' Mum said sarcastically as she pressed her face next to mine and we tried to blow out the sparklers, which of course was impossible.

Two weeks later we were again giggling at our frequenting of 'high end' establishments as we sat at McDonald's, celebrating my daughter McKenzie's seventh birthday with her cousins and aunties. It was a far cry from her sixth birthday party at home with fifteen children, colour-coordinated everything and the cake that I had spent hours making. Good thing we all loved the golden arches; Mum could inhale a quarter pounder stuffed with all the pickles that the children didn't want, and had even adopted my youngest brother's disgusting habit of putting fries inside the burger.

She wore Raisin Pearl

Without even realising it, we had transitioned from the daily fear that Mum was dying from cancer to a more accepting stance that she was simply living with cancer. The regular appointments no longer prompted nervous anticipation; they had become part of our routine. That was, until the day Dr John delivered news we hadn't expected so soon. 'The tumour markers are on the rise and there is no other suitable chemotherapy for you. I'm afraid there is nothing left to try.'

It was the second time we had heard an oncologist indicate all options had been exhausted. I knew I'd already pushed my luck with Mum by getting her to change specialists – there was no way she would be interested in looking around for another expert. But where did that leave us? I couldn't bring myself to acknowledge that we had reached the end of the line. Mum sat in silence as I grasped at ways to find her a detour to death's door. The previous oncologist had said that there were no trials Mum would be eligible for but it didn't stop me asking Dr John the same question.

'What about a trial drug? Isn't there someone somewhere looking for volunteers? We have nothing to lose.'

'It's worth a try. I will make some calls and see what's available,' he said.

Not all hope was lost but we left with an uneasy feeling defeat was in the air. I was annoyed at myself for having eased the intense focus we had begun the cancer journey with, and felt like I had wasted precious time not maintaining my active research into sourcing medical trials around the world. Mentally I made a list of people I planned to call that might be able to help, friends who were medical journalists who could point me in the right direction.

Forty-eight hours later Mum mentioned in passing that her stomach was bloated. She wasn't alarmed and assumed it was fluid retention but over the next three days the swelling became quite obvious on her small frame. We knew it was better to play it safe and made an appointment to have some tests in hospital the following day.

I was watching the clock in the waiting room as it ticked twenty-five minutes past our scheduled time and knew the delay was going to wreak havoc with traffic and school pick-up time. 'You go,' Mum ordered. 'I hate it when you're late to pick up the kids, it upsets them. I will ring you when I'm in my room.'

She called before I'd even made it to the school.

'Gee that was quick!' I said.

'I'm in a taxi on my way home,' was the reply.

'What do you mean? The doctor said he would keep you in for a few days.'

'I know, I know, but they have said that I've got gas and sent me on my way.'

'Go back, Mum. I'll ring the doctor, you need to be admitted.'

'Too late, I'm almost home.'

It turned out there was a misunderstanding. The next day I took Mum back to the same hospital and she was admitted for monitoring. Three days later we were none the wiser, though she was richer for the experience and had even befriended the nurses who helped satisfy her craving for the 'golden arches'. One of them during their break walked fifty metres down the road to McDonald's and delivered a quarter pounder to her bedside. Her mood was upbeat and relaxed when I paid her a visit.

'I dreamt of your funeral last night,' I confessed.

'Yes, I've dreamt about it too,' she said. 'The kids were gathered around the casket and throughout the service they decorated it with lovely drawings.'

I started to laugh. 'Nice idea, Mum, in theory, but you know what little kids are like and we have a fair few toddlers in our lot. It would all start out well and then one would want the colour another had, there would be a squabble and a tug of war for the colour and before you know it, the coffin would take a hit and Nana would come rolling out.'

I thought my dream was more practical. 'In my dream all the grandchildren had decorated love-heart cut-outs and then during the service they stuck them on the casket.'

'I like my dream better,' Mum said with a faint smile.

With no real idea of what was the problem she was released from hospital. The words 'gas' and 'fluid' were bandied around but there was nothing conclusive, and neither sounded sinister, though in a phone conversation Dr John confirmed my fear that the downhill slide had indeed begun. I pressed him for what that meant. How long did we have?

'I would think between eight and twelve weeks, although given your mother's fighting spirit I wouldn't be surprised if she lasted longer.'

In my mind I madly began converting weeks to months. Two or three months was November at best, if her fighting spirit kicked in maybe Christmas, but by then she would be on borrowed time and what state would she be in? Just a few weeks earlier I'd had no doubt Mum would see at least one more festive season, maybe even two, but in a matter of a few days such hopes all but disintegrated. The estimate meant we had already had our last Christmas together, we just hadn't known it at the time. Had we made it special enough? Shit, I couldn't remember.

With November seemingly an unlikely goal I began working backwards to calculate the events she would still be alive for. Baby James's first birthday in September was within reach, and Robert and Sharon's baby Bentley was due then too. She would certainly hang on for that, I was sure of it.

'What about our health-farm getaway?' I asked. Our precious mother-daughter time was just over two weeks away. 'Yes, I think she will be OK,' said Dr John. 'I would encourage you to press ahead with your plans, it will be good for her.'

When I arrived to collect Mum from the ward, she was dressed, lipstick on and ready to leave. She always made a point of saying goodbye and thank you to the nurses who'd taken care of her. It had been four days since she had seen the kids. It felt like a lifetime for her and them and there were demands from them all for a 'welcome home' afternoon tea. The love in the room lasted about forty-five minutes before one sibling began squabbling with another over coloured pencils and that was the cue to leave.

'How about I take the kids home, feed them and later I will bring down the moussaka I've made.'

'Sounds great.' She laughed and waved us all off down the street.

When I returned the house was as warm as toast, soft lights were on and she had a glass of red wine waiting for me. The two of us ate and pondered the events of the last few days in hospital, which still didn't seem to add up. Then I remembered Mum's old habit of withholding the truth in an effort to protect me.

'Are you sure there isn't something you're not telling me about what happened in hospital? Did they actually use the words "fluid" or "gas"? Or is that what you've decided to tell me?

'I promise! That's exactly what they told me.'

'Well your track record of telling the truth on serious health matters is not that flash. I will be really pissed off if you're holding out on me.'

'On my dying word of honour.'

'Yeah, well, we know when you're dead that won't count for much.'

I knew it wouldn't have mattered if she'd sworn black and blue that she wasn't withholding information, I still wasn't convinced and planned to crosscheck with Dr John. My thoughts were broken by Mum speaking hers.

'I've been thinking. I want you to have all my jewellery.'

'What?'

It was a bombshell I hadn't expected – not just at that moment but ever.

From the time I used to play dress-up and parade around in Mum's fur coats and heels I'd adorn myself with her strings of pearls, rings and other bits and bobs. I knew one day most of it would be mine because I was the only girl. The only items that were to be divided among my brothers and I were the five strings of pearls. One had a diamond clasp, another had gold links from my great-grandfather's fob watch, and a topaz shamrock hung off another. Some had been handed down from several generations and were in their original form, others had been remodelled during a stage Mum had gone through twenty-odd years ago when just about everything she owned was 'reworked'. My whole life Mum had made her wishes crystal clear: 'When I die each son will receive a string of pearls; if they choose they can pass it on to their wives or daughters.'

This wish wasn't in her will, it didn't need to be. It was good as set in stone in all our minds. Now she was changing it.

'Ah, no thanks,' I said, holding up my hand. 'You can't do that, that's not the deal.'

'Because you're my only daughter! I've decided it won't mean nearly as much to anyone as it does to you. You have three daughters, all of whom will have memories of me. The pearls are not really worth much but they will mean much more to them. Anyway, that's what I've decided.'

'Well that just great, Mum! How to start a family rift before you're even gone.'

'It's what I want to do.'

'Then you have to tell the boys, and don't even dream of leaving me to explain that one when you're gone. It's got nothing to do with me.'

And that was the end of that topic. The jewellery had clearly been on her 'to do' list and now it was done.

'Because you're my daughter'. I used to loathe that line because it was delivered with increasing regularity from the time I reached double figures, but in a different context.

'Why am I the one who has to help with ironing shirts when my brothers get to iron handkerchiefs for fun?'

'Why do they wash the cars and I have to do the vacuuming or hang washing on the line?'

'Why don't I rake the leaves and they peel potatoes?'

I know Mum thought it was preparing me for life but to me it just seemed a gender handicap. Somehow 'because you're my daughter' left an unwanted imprint on me: even long after she'd stopped saying it I would think it. My mother firmly believed in the old adage: 'A son is your son till he finds him a wife, a daughter is your daughter for the rest of your life.' As for the mother-daughter relationship, she was wise enough to know that she would have to bide her time until I would truly grasp its gift and responsibilities. Negative connotations of that line dissolved with the years, replaced with a deep appreciation of and gratitude at being her only girl.

A lump caught in my throat as my memories and the conversation about her jewellery reminded me that in the not-too-distant future I would cease to be the 'only' daughter: I would be no one's daughter.

We resumed idle chitchat about what spa treatments we would book for our getaway at the health retreat and what she had planned for the next day. Robert and Sharon and two-year-old son Harley were coming up from the coast to see her. I finished my wine and walked home worrying about the possible fallout from Mum's change of heart on the jewellery, which could become 'Pearlgate'.

There was no indication that our cancer journey was about to take a dramatic turn. I was confident that there would be a gradual descent that would allow us to prepare. I was wrong. Just twelve hours later the direction we were headed was south.

She wore Plum Velour

It was just after dawn, Sunday morning, August 1st. A winter morning required at least two cups of tea before anything else could be done. I had just started dishing out cereal to the children when it occurred to me that I hadn't heard from Mum yet. In the past few months we had gotten into the habit of letting her ring me after she woke. If the morning call was late I knew that she was feeling nauseous or fatigued and needed rest, and that she'd call me when she was up to it.

I suspected she would sleep in that morning because she'd be enjoying the comfort of her own bed after her few days in a hospital bed. The phone rang at about eleven.

'Ah, you're finally awake!' I said, but it wasn't Mum, it was Robert.'

'Where is Mum? We're on our way up to see her and I've tried calling several times but there's no answer.'

'She's at home or she should be. I hope she is …'

I hung up and started ringing her also, but it rang out. I immediately hit redial. The phone was answered but all I heard was a faint whisper.

'Hello.'

'Mum, I'm coming down.'

A cold shudder went through me as I ran out the door and down the street. I could see my brother pulling up outside her house.

'Stay there for a minute,' I yelled to him. I let myself in and dreaded what I would find. Mum was lying in her nightdress on the floor in the hallway. She was conscious but weak and more than a little annoyed that her bladder had given way. I reasoned that if she was annoyed she couldn't be too bad.

'Geez, Mum, what happened? How long have you been lying here?'

'An hour or so I think. I was walking to the kitchen to make a cup of tea but my legs gave way. I knew you would come to find me sooner or later, but I don't want the boys to see me like this.'

'You've got the phone beside you, why didn't you call me?'

'It was early, I didn't want to wake you.'

'But Robert has been trying to call, you didn't answer.'

'I must have dozed off.'

I helped Mum up, changed her nightdress and got her back into bed. She was lethargic and pale but was more concerned about me cleaning the small soil on the carpet before anyone came.

My big brother's face was etched with worry as he came through the front door.

'What's going on? Is Mum all right?'

'She's OK but she had a fall on the way to the kitchen and she's embarrassed. Go and grab a coffee and come back, but you might want to send Sharon and Harley to the park, Mum isn't up to it today.'

Robert returned half an hour later. 'Harley is very worried about you, Mum. He's been yelling in the car, "Why can't I see Nana?"'

Whilst they talked I picked up the phone and rang the doctor's after-hours number and explained what had happened. He suggested we make an appointment for Tuesday.

'Ah really? Today is Sunday, something is clearly wrong, how about before Tuesday?' I asked.

He agreed to send a nurse to the house that day to take blood samples.

'I rang Mick, he'll be here soon,' Robert announced. 'And I rang Steve in Queensland, he's back tomorrow.'

'Really, there's no need for everyone to rush over, it's just that my legs won't do what I want them to, I just need rest,' Mum reassured us.

The overnight decline made no sense. Little about the last few days did. A week earlier she'd been at McDonald's eating chocolate fudge sundaes for her granddaughter's birthday, taking happy snaps, and suddenly it seemed like the curtain was coming down. Despite Mum's declaration that she was feeling OK, I had a sinking feeling that a fast-forward button had been pushed and we were at the beginning of the end. I wasn't ready.

The dramatic shift from being able-bodied to not being able to bear her own weight meant Mum would need almost twenty-four-hour support. The concept didn't sit well with her and she was frustrated that her 'mind over matter' attitude wasn't going to help her get to the kitchen or even to the toilet without some assistance.

Once my brother Mick arrived it was agreed we would need to take turns to stay over with Mum at the very least until the results from the blood tests came back and we knew what we were dealing with.

'I'll stay tonight,' Mick volunteered.

He slept on the couch, helped Mum to the bathroom in the morning before he left for work, and I arrived half an hour later with James after school drop-off.

'I hate this, I hate being needy,' she grumbled.

'Well I'm sorry about that,' I replied with no apology at all. 'There's not much else we can do. It's not like you have to ask your sons to wipe your bum, you can still do that, it's just getting you there. I will be able to do everything else.'

After I helped her into the shower I decided to stand there to make sure she didn't fall. As she closed her eyes and let the water fall down her back, offering warm relief, I could tell she was frustrated by her failing body and loss of independence.

'Oh, thank God!' I said into the phone when the doctor explained that it wasn't the cancer that had struck Mum down but a virus she'd caught during her hospital stay. The bug had gone through the ward and several other patients had been affected too, but it had hit Mum harder because her immune system was already low from the chemotherapy. The doctor warned that it could take several days for her to recover and suggested we reschedule our appointment to see him for the following week.

The word 'recover' lifted my spirits. Mum was going to recover from being bedridden and I allowed myself to board the emotional rollercoaster as it moved out of the bottom dip and up again. Looking at Mum lying in bed whilst I spoke to the doctor, there was no denying how hard the virus had hit and I voiced my concerns about her being well enough to go on our trip. To my surprise he still thought we should proceed as planned.

'I'll be right by then,' Mum insisted. 'I wasn't all that fussed about going but now I'm really looking forward to it.' I could see she was determined to go, and really she just had to be fit to fly – and she would be, even if she had to be in a wheelchair.

Steve arrived home from Queensland with his bag packed for a week. It was fortuitous that his stay had been planned months ago whilst his wife Vink and kids Matthew and Emily remained interstate with her parents. They were killing a few days before moving into a new house, but their new address was only one street down from their old house, still within walking distance to mine and to Mum.

Mum's care was relatively easy to manage but she was still frustrated at having to be waited on hand and foot. There was hesitation in her voice when she asked for a drink or something to eat, and it was apparent she didn't want to trouble anyone even if that person was me. The blow-up mattress was put in the sewing room just across the hall and Mum could ring Steve's mobile if she needed anything during the night: the phone was the only way to wake Steve once he fell asleep. I knew she would still try to hold off going to the toilet on his watch, and though perhaps it was awkward for them both the first time, by the third night it was just accepted as part of what needed to be done, though she would never get used to it.

It became a loose tag team that somehow just worked. Steve would go to work and Mum was fine alone for an hour or so until I arrived after the morning school drop, and then baby James and I would spend the day with her, nipping out here and there to do errands or pick-ups.

After two days of doing nothing but sleep, Mum was desperate to see my girls. 'I miss the babies, I hate not seeing them, can you bring them in just to say hello on your way home from school?'

McKenzie, Sidney and Stella had been asking when they could see Nana, and whilst I knew Mum wasn't up to her standard afternoon tea offering I figured five minutes was better than nothing. The brief interlude was an injection of happiness and pure love that no drug could match and gave her a reason to brush her hair and put on lipstick. The bright colour was an instant lift to her pale face and provided a protective shield for the children, masking the growing reality.

'Oh, Nana, I like your lipstick,' McKenzie said.

'Are you OK, Nana?' was as serious as the enquiry about her health got. We were there long enough for them to give Nana a kiss and quick rundown of their day, she let them choose a lolly from her stash beside the bed and then we left.

'Bye, Nana, love you, see you tomorrow.'

Steve was back at Mum's house each day by five pm and I would return after witching hour at my house, leaving my husband to read stories and put the kids to bed. The other brothers were dropping in at various times; there was always someone coming and going if she needed anything. It was all made so much easier by me living fifty metres away. I lost count of how many times I said to her, 'Good thing we moved you into this house, Mum.'

'Best thing we ever did,' she agreed.

It was a very long five days before Mum began to improve. She was still sleeping a lot during the day but not for hours on end, a little colour had returned to her face and she was able to eat small amounts. There was no sign that her legs were regaining any strength but no one really expected that yet, and the small improvement was enough to prompt her suggestion to have a family dinner.

As I helped Mum shuffle into the kitchen the gentle family banter continued. The mood felt heavy though no one needed to verbally acknowledge it.

Mick had been in charge of the dinner and had produced his culinary best, tacos. The table wasn't big enough to seat everyone so we all stood, including Mum, who had refused a chair and chose instead to stand alongside us. Maybe she had already registered that the casual gathering was likely to be among the final family dinners we would ever have. She pushed herself beyond her limit to join in, though despite her determination to stay focused she seemed to fade out at times. For many years the matriarch of our family had been dwarfed by her three sons, who all pushed through six foot, but that night she looked small and frail. It was clear she had no appetite, but she was there, her children were beside her and that was all that mattered.

'Well, I'm going to save Nana with this juice,' announced Robert and pulled a bottle of dark purple liquid from a bag. 'Jungle juice,' he declared.

It wasn't actually called jungle juice but frankly we didn't really care what the official name was. Robert knew someone who had bought it for a relative with cancer, who had since gone into remission.

'This has come from America, it's not released here yet. Thirty mils three times a day.' And with that he was pouring Mum her first shot. The air in the room suddenly felt lighter as we all filled our glasses with wine and hope. If there was a chance the 'jungle juice' could give Mum more time, perhaps even more time to get her onto a medical trial, then we were going for it.

'Let's do it,' Mum said with conviction, and drank what might well have been nothing more than fruit juice. There was nothing to lose.

'And we're back, Nana's on her way back,' one of my brothers said, raising his glass.

Within an hour the outing away from her bed had taken its toll. I helped her shuffle slowly back to bed and she fell asleep to the familiar noises of her children and a busy kitchen.

Perhaps Mum had convinced herself that the 'jungle juice' worked overnight, or maybe she was willing her ailing body to respond. Whichever it was, the next morning after school drop-off I walked into her house and immediately saw that she wasn't in bed. With my heart racing into overdrive I ran into her ensuite and found her lying on the bathroom floor with a towel over her. As soon as I saw that she wasn't hurt I got angry.

'Mum? Didn't you learn from last time?'

'I'm sorry,' she said apologetically

In a stubborn attempt to reclaim some sense of dignity she had waited until Steve left for work and then walked the five steps to the toilet. Who knows how long it had taken her.

'I was feeling OK. I thought I'd be all right and I was, but when I tried to get up off the toilet my legs gave out.'

Whilst her body had failed her foresight hadn't. She'd been able to reach the switch of the small blow heater on the floor, turned it on then pulled a towel from the hanging rail and covered herself to keep warm, knowing I would arrive within the hour.

My annoyance was replaced by despair after I tried to lift her up under the arms. I could barely move her. Mum had no use of her legs at all.

'Well what the hell do we do now?' I scolded her. Mum was little and light but lifting forty-three kilos was going to be no mean feat. The biggest problem was that she had zero strength and couldn't help me in any way; she was basically dead weight. I knew I simply had to find a way to get her back to bed. I couldn't leave her there until help arrived. She was still a private woman with immense pride and it wasn't going to be stripped from her on my watch.

It was obvious I had broken every OH&S rule ever made on my first attempt but I had reacted on impulse rather than with any regard for my back. I could never have imagined how difficult it would be; she couldn't even grab onto the bath to help boost herself up. The frustration was excruciating for her.

'I'm sorry, I am no help to you whatsoever, absolutely bloody useless.'

On a second attempt I crouched behind her, locked my elbows under her armpits and in several moves carefully dragged her backwards across the tiles and carpet to the bed. We paused for a few minutes for me to catch my breath before deciding what to do next. In a third manoeuvre I somehow lifted her torso face down up onto the edge of the bed, leaning against her so she didn't slip back down, and finally swung her legs up and over. I will never know how I managed it but I did, and have a hernia to prove it. The whole episode took a lot out of us both and soon after she dozed off.

Walking was impossible. She could stand with assistance but that was all. The nurse arrived mid morning to take blood and arranged for a shower frame and commode to be delivered to the house. It arrived just a few hours later, along with a wheelchair. The mere presence of those 'aides' that kept catching my eye from every angle of the bedroom made me feel sad. We were losing the battle.

I rang the doctor in search of an explanation as to why Mum was feeling better but her legs were getting worse. He explained that he had increased the dose of one of her drugs in an attempt to keep her liver functioning at an acceptable level in the event she was able to get on a cancer trial program. The vital drug was called dexamethasone. It was basically keeping her alive but the payoff for buying more time was that in return for her mobility we had traded the muscles in her legs.

Just when I thought the rollercoaster of emotions had sunk to a new low and wouldn't recover I found my spirits being lifted again as I reasoned that the physical deterioration was medically induced and served a purpose. I relayed the information to Mum but her lacklustre response showed that she derived no comfort from the explanation; walking came under her 'quality of life' criterion. Despite my pledge to acknowledge and accept when it was time to give up I knew my goal posts had shifted. I no longer cared if she never walked again, I just wanted her to live, and if the jungle juice kicked in and there was a trial drug available then there was still a chance. I was holding onto that thought, visualising it, willing the universe to make it happen, until the doctor rang early that afternoon. The news was all bad.

'I'm afraid Pam has been knocked back for the cancer trial program I was hoping to get her on.' No reason was given other than that she simply wasn't a suitable candidate, and I had no medical knowledge to help me ask the right questions or argue her case. The knocks kept coming. The latest blood results showed those damn cancer markers had shot through the roof and confirmed what we had already been told: the treatment was no longer keeping the tumours steady, and they were increasing their assault on Mum's liver. A domino effect had begun and the vital organ that the body relies on to flush out toxins had started to falter, causing her ammonia levels to head skywards.

'What will high levels of ammonia do?' I asked.

The doctor spoke of fatigue, loss of appetite and forgetfulness. I realised that Mum had been showing these signs for several days but I'd passed them off as the fallout from the virus she had contracted.

'There is one other trial I have applied to get Pam on but for her even to be considered we have to get her ammonia levels down.'

In an instant my emotions were back on the rollercoaster, and rather than focus on the knockback I chose to tell Mum about the trial that might be possible if her ammonia levels could be reduced.

If I had chosen to listen more closely to what my mother wasn't saying I might have been forced to acknowledge her slight shift away from what had been a united fight. She was no longer showing an openness to try alternatives to fight for her life, which is probably why I made no attempt to gauge her interest in the latest trial, because to do so might have given her the opportunity to say no. Among the doctor's suggestions of how to reduce ammonia levels my ears only heard that sugar blocks ammonia, and though I knew I shouldn't, as soon as I hung up the phone I was on the computer Googling 'ways to block ammonia in the body'. It was pointless trying food options as Mum was past eating proper meals; I needed to find something that required little effort on her part. Somewhere in the searches I found that good snacks included jellybeans. Mum loved jellybeans and was one of the few people I'd ever known to like the black ones. Within fifteen minutes I was on my way to the pharmacy to buy five packets.

'Right, Mum, you're going start to popping these – there's a trial you might get on if we can get your ammonia levels down.'

She said nothing but her raised eyebrows and deadpan facial expression screamed, 'You think that's going to do it, do you?'

I took no notice and handed her two jellybeans, and continued to do so at frequent intervals. I would jest that it was important to mix up the colour combinations, and every time she gave me the same look that said, 'You're kidding yourself.' I was aware that Mum didn't for one moment believe the sweets would make a difference, that she was simply humouring me, but I figured I had enough energy to fight and carry both of us and until she actually told me to stop then I was going to exhaust every likely and unlikely possibility.

She wore Rich Raisin Frost

I feel good,' Mum said the next morning, but her statement was delivered with a little too much enthusiasm for me really to believe her. She was already propped up high on her pillow when I arrived and compared to the last few days was looking fantastic.

'See, it's the jungle juice and jellybeans,' I mocked, and headed straight to the kitchen to pour her a shot of the dark purple juice and make tea.

Her marked improvement was a boost to everyone's spirits and we were still hopeful that she would be accepted onto a different trial drug program, but after the events of the day before I didn't want to delay the conversation we needed to have about the imminent need for twenty-four-hour care. Steve had been a wonderful night watchman but he had a business to run, his family were about to return from interstate and they would be flat out moving house. We were all ready to pitch in and do whatever was needed but no one knew how long Mum would need the high level of care; it could be weeks or months. The reality was that all her children had work commitments and/or very young children; we were going to need additional help and Mum needed to decide whom she was willing for that to be.

There was no shortage of offers. Word of Mum's rapid decline had filtered through the neighbourhood and there was a steady stream of text messages and telephone calls from Mum's close friends and relatives.

'Please tell Pammie we are thinking of her.'

'Do you need anything?'

'If I can do anything to help please just pick up the phone.'

I passed on every single message and Mum was genuinely touched. 'That's lovely of them to offer.'

Mum was aware that the care she was going to need would be intimate and confronting. It was a big thing to ask of anyone, even if they had willingly volunteered, and as instructed all offers were politely refused.

'If you want to stay at home I need real help, Mum. Mary-Ann wants to do it and I think you should let her.'

Mum quickly batted the idea away. 'I know Mary-Ann says she wants to help but she has a full-time job and she doesn't have any annual leave owing.'

Mum's sister Mary-Ann was a principal at a local primary school and she was completely dedicated to her job. Her love of children inside and outside the classroom was effortlessly part of her character and she'd been an intricate thread throughout our lives.

Aunty Mary-Ann was the fun aunt, ten years younger than Mum, a redhead with an infectious laugh who had time and a lolly for her nephews and nieces. 'Mare' was the one running the games at our childhood birthday parties, never failing to involve even the most reluctant guest in a game of What's the Time, Mr Wolf? Her energy and enthusiasm didn't wane even when she had children of her own or with the passing years; she still had the energy to run all the games at my children's parties.

Apart from sharing the same shoe size, Mare and Mum were opposites: red hair to the other's blonde, olive skin to fair, tall to short. Mare was highly educated but Mum knew how to run a business; Mare was the life of any party, her sister liked to stand back; Mum was on time for everything, Mare was permanently running late. They were a perfect yin and yang and had always been close, and their relationship as sisters dualed as a mother-daughter relationship after the death of their mother when Mary-Ann was still in her early twenties. There was ebb and flow at different stages, but they always found time for one another. It was no surprise that Mary-Ann wanted to care for her big sister, nor was it a surprise that Mum was worried Mare didn't have annual leave to spare.

Sitting on Mum's bed, I rang Mary-Ann to engage in a pointless debate. For Mary-Ann it was a fait accompli. 'I have taken long-service leave. I will come down this afternoon and every day at any time of day to do whatever you want me to, it doesn't matter if it's taking the kids to school or making cups of tea, I want to be there.' And that was that! I knew I had secured the best possible wingman and allowed myself to exhale a little, though I wasn't done with my recruiting. My next suggestion was not going to sit well with Mum.

'I'd like to ask Jayne to help too. Mary-Ann and I can do most of it but Jayne's nursing background means she has the medical knowledge.' Jayne and Mum hadn't been friends for long but friendship need not be measured by longevity.

We had all met when my brother Robert bought a beach house next door to Jayne and her family, and had enjoyed many fun informal gatherings. We shared their shock and sadness when Jayne's husband fell ill three years later and admired her determination to nurse him at home until his last breath just a few months after he had been diagnosed. Over the next five years an uncomplicated, respectful friendship based on similar life circumstances and interests gently developed between Jayne and my mother. Neither of them had any desire to re-partner and both were happy devoting themselves to their children's growing families. They would often catch a movie together and have lunch or dinner afterwards, and would also go to markets near and far, trawling for materials for little girls' dresses and items for their grandchildren's fairy gardens.

Jayne had already offered to help in any way but I could sense she was wary of overstepping the mark; Mum conversely didn't want to ask too much of her friend. 'It's only a few years since she nursed her husband, I don't know if you can ask anyone to do it again, and she's busy with her own family, they need her too,' said Mum.

I pondered whether Jayne would feel able to say no if she felt it was too much too soon. The past few days had given me a glimpse of how all-consuming it was nursing a terminally ill patient. How long could we ask anyone outside the family to help sustain that level of care?

There was only one way to find out, and when Jayne dropped past later that day I broached the subject

'I understand if this is too difficult for you, but …'

Her reply was emphatic. 'Of course I will help in any way you want me to. I'd be honoured.'

It was comforting to have my 'A' team on standby, knowing I could call on them when needed, and I genuinely thought that was all that would be needed until a nurse from palliative care came by that afternoon. It was the same chap we had enjoyed a casual chat with in Mum's kitchen six months earlier. I wondered whether despite our optimism back then his experience had told him it wouldn't be long before his return.

'We're here to support you. Why don't we organise for a nurse to drop by every day?'

My immediate reaction was to resist. Mum was improving ever so slightly and a daily visit from a nurse felt akin to waving the white flag, and we weren't yet – well, I wasn't. In a kind and gentle manner he reassured me that some days there might be no need for a nurse but that it was easier to have the visit in place in the event that Mum was having a bad day.

'Pamela, you might also want to consider coming into the hospice if caring becomes difficult at home. It doesn't have to be permanent, even just a few days.'

Well, that was one topic I wasn't going to be swayed on – I had made a promise. 'No. Mum wants to be at home, I want her at home. I have my aunt and a friend who is a nurse to help me.'

'That's fine,' he said, 'it's just an option available to you if you want it. Now, Pamela, is there anything I can do for you?'

'I want it to be quick.' Six words that said it all.

Mum was tired; the morning brightness had now deserted her and she was drifting off. The nurse and I moved to the kitchen to run through the long list of pills I was administering.

'This is a very high dose of dexamethasone, we can reduce this now,' he suggested.

The names of all the other pills meant little to me but I knew dexamethasone was key and decided to come clean on our intentions.

'We don't want to change the dose because we're trying to get Mum on a trial drug program. I'll reduce it when Mum tells me to. That time isn't now.'

I'm not sure if he agreed with our decision but he moved on without a hint of disapproval or judgement, and as I showed him out he reassured me that assistance was available 24/7.

'He is a nice man, I like him,' Mum said when she woke.

'It takes a special kind of person to be able to do that for a living.'

Fatigue forced its dominant hand for most of the afternoon and the house was mostly quiet but for the radio station playing all my parents' old favourites. The Carpenters' song 'We've Only Just Begun' came on; it made me melancholy and as I pottered around the warm home Mum had made her own I felt just a little teary that there would be no new beginnings for her.

Before the sun had set the brothers arrived armed with red wine. After greeting Mum with a kiss they began to size up one another's offerings, deciding which one to open, but first the ribbing began.

'Gee you lashed out on this drop,' said one.

'I see you didn't,' said another.

'Oh he's got plenty of money, let's drink his first! Someone get the glasses.'

The familiar sound of sibling banter and jibes echoing around her were an immediate boost for Mum, who suddenly found energy to join in the conversation.

'You want a wicky, Nana?' quipped Robert, referring to what had become our family's name for whisky.

'I wish I felt like one.' Mum smiled though her tone was sad.

A half-measure of scotch and soda with lots of ice had long been her choice of drink. One day some four years earlier I had walked into a bottle shop with my two little girls in a pram when to my amusement and embarrassment one of them asked very loudly, 'Do you want red wine or white wine, Mum? And don't forget some wicky for Nana.' From then on that's what Mum's favourite tipple was referred to as, even though she hadn't touched one for the best part of two years.

'Have you been taking the jungle juice, Nana?' Robert wanted to know, pouring an extra shotglass of the dark purple liquid for good measure.

'Yeees,' Mum moaned. 'And jellybeans. Kel has been giving me jungle juice and jellybeans every time I look at her.'

Eyebrows were raised as I explained the method behind my jellybean madness and my hope it would bring down Mum's ammonia levels.

'You're kidding yourself,' one brother scoffed as he topped up the wine glasses.

I updated everyone on the palliative-care visit and we made a verbal roster of who was going to stay over on what night.

'It's such a pain for everyone,' Mum said once again.

Telling her not to worry was pointless, the new status quo of her being reliant on others for everything would never sit well with her.

Before the night ended I reminded Mum that her girlfriend from the country would be coming the next day for a few hours; she had called several times over the last week wanting to help. I'd mentioned it to Mum each time she rang but her answer had been the same.

'I don't want anyone here. I don't want to have to make conversation.'

I felt bad every time I declined the offer because I knew it was more about a friend who really needed to say goodbye without necessarily having to say it.

'I will just come and read my book, she doesn't need to talk to me,' Mum's friend said in another phone call, and so I put it to Mum a final time.

'Come on, Mum, she just wants to sit for a while.'

'OK,' she surrendered.

When Mum's friend arrived on that sunny Sunday afternoon, she was true to her word. With book in hand she propped herself on the soft couch in Mum's bedroom whilst my brothers and I tended to the usual round of young family life: shopping, washing, party drop-offs and playdates. When I returned a few hours later she was in a chair next to Mum's bed still reading her book. Mum was sleeping.

There had been little talk between the two. Mum had indeed slept most of the time, but I did learn that at one point she woke briefly and out of the blue requested that her friend clean out the fridge.

'She asked you to clean out the fridge?' I asked, somewhat bemused, wondering whether the drugs might have been having some strange side effect.

'Yes. She asked me to go through it and pitch everything. She didn't want any old food in there and thought you would all be too busy to do it.'

I couldn't help but giggle at the absurdity of the request and yet knew it was so typical of Mum. Nothing ever gathered dust in her fridge; there was only ever fresh produce at its prime. 'If in doubt, throw it out,' was her motto. The fact that she was even thinking about her fridge status at this point was strangely amusing. We all had a checklist of things that needed to be done in these crucial days, but only Mum would have the fridge on hers. At least it was done now.

By early evening the siblings had once again assembled and red wine was liberally poured. We took up various positions in Mum's room and she grabbed hold of bite-size snippets of wakefulness.

'So when do you see the doctor again, Mum?' asked Mick.

'Tuesday,' I answered for her. It was only two days away but I felt like it would never come.

The conversation shifted to light banter about the boys' working week and Steve's pending house move, and I could feel Mum relax, enjoying being surrounded by her children. We could all sense that she was trying desperately hard to stay awake to grasp the simple pleasure but it wasn't long before her eyes gave into the weight forcing them shut. Wine glasses were soon drained and everyone made their exit, leaving Steve to begin another night shift.

The next morning at the changing of the guard I felt both hopeful and apprehensive as I began to plan for Tuesday's make-or-break meeting with Dr John. The logistics of getting Mum to the oncologist's appointment seemed straightforward enough. We had a wheelchair to transport her from the house to the car and then into hospital and Mary-Ann had insisted on coming along to help. It was only later in the afternoon that I realised we had no way to get the wheelchair down the steps from the house to the car; I knew I couldn't lift Mum.

As I tried to think of ways around the problem I recalled a mum from school whose husband had built a ramp for their newborn's cot to move easily around their house. I was hopeful they still had it.

'Yes we sure do,' was the reply when I rang to ask. 'I'll send him around with it after dinner.'

Steve and I were having a glass of red when the man arrived with the ramp. He placed it over the steps, but as I attempted to roll the wheelchair down the ramp it was clear we had another problem.

'Shit! The wheelchair is too wide,' I said.

It was only five centimetres out but it might as well have been a metre. It was not going to help me get Mum to the car.

'Thanks anyway, mate, it was really nice of you to bring it around,' Steve said, and we bade him farewell.

Mum was sleeping and we resumed our positions in the living room.

'I can come home from work and lift Mum into the car,' Steve suggested.

'Yes, well, that only fixes half the problem. What happens when we get back from the appointment a few hours later?'

'Well, I guess I will just come back.'

I was convinced there had to be another option. 'Maybe Mary-Ann and I can lift Mum,' I said. 'She's too heavy for me but two of us could manage it.'

It was around nine pm when I received an SMS on my phone.

'You up?'

A few minutes later the man with the ramp was on the doorstep. The father of four, who had worked all day and whom we had only met a few times, had gone home and, instead of sitting down with his wife, had got out his tools and made the ramp wider.

I could feel a lump lodge in my throat as he laid down the adjusted ramp and I pushed the wheelchair down it. 'It's perfect.'

I could see Steve's gratitude as he warmly shook his hand. 'Thanks, mate'.

'No worries at all, see ya later.'

It was a gesture I found so completely overwhelming that after he left I closed the door and couldn't help but weep.

'Shit, I'm about to cry too,' my brother said in jest, though I knew he wasn't joking.

We shared another glass of red and for the next ten minutes sang the praises of the man we hardly knew but would never ever forget.

She wore Black Cherry

D-day had arrived. Her lips were perfectly painted a rich, strong colour. Mary-Ann had helped Mum get dressed and when I walked through the door just after school drop-off she was sitting in the wheelchair, wig on, a full face of make-up, her birthday winter jacket on ready to go.

I'd stopped at our local cake shop and bought one of Mum's favourites, a coffee éclair. It was the perfect pick-me-up: fluffy choux pastry pumped with fresh whipped cream and a sliver of coffee-flavoured icing on top. There was complete silence as Mum devoured it.

'Nothing can come between Pammie and those damn éclairs,' Mary-Ann chortled.

It was time to go. The ramp was in place but it was then I realised we hadn't considered how to get from the living room through the kitchen and laundry to the back door. With no experience in manoeuvring a wheelchair or navigating tight doorways and corners, we fumbled our way through ten-point turns, scraping a few skirting boards just to get to the ramp. I was relieved that Mum was able to bear some of her own weight for a few seconds as we helped her from the chair. Mary-Ann then pulled the chair back so Mum was able to shuffle a small turn and ease into the front seat, and we lifted her legs inside.

I got behind the wheel of Mum's black hatchback, which she and the kids had nicknamed 'the Little Ripper' and moved the seat back to give me more leg room. I felt a fleeting moment of sadness, noting that I was adjusting Mum's setting, probably forever.

'Right!' I said. 'Who would have thought that getting you into the car was going to be a production? I'm exhausted and we haven't even left home yet.'

'Well, I was no help to you at all. Useless, absolutely useless,' said Mum with what had become a familiar air of frustration.

'Thank goodness you could stand a little otherwise we would have been two degrees of stuffed – just as well you had that éclair; the sugar hit gave you the energy.'

'Those cakes are bloody faaaantastic,' Mare chimed in from the back seat.

As we drove along the main road to the hospital I felt Mum reach out and hold my hand. It wasn't unusual for her to do that following a meaningful conversation, a gesture that would convey support, pride or an understanding, but there were no words. I wondered whether her hold meant 'I'm scared' or 'This is it' – maybe it was a little of both.

'Oh, I've forgotten my lipstick,' said Mare. 'What have you got in your bag, Pammie? I'll just use one of yours.'

There must have been two or three shades rolling around in the black bag.

'Million Dollar Red. That will do me; I could do with a million dollars. Do you want some, Kel?'

'No I've got some on.'

Mare laughed. 'Who cares, put some more on. A million dollars mixes well with everything.'

We were as ready as we could ever be for what was about to come.

We made our way into the elevator and pushed the button that lit up for level one. As we felt the pull upward I stared at the unlit button for level two and was reminded how the hospital, until recent months, had held only happy memories. It was where my obstetrician's rooms were and on level two was where I had delivered one of my four children and also where the other three grandchildren had been born. What a difference a floor level makes. The doors opened and we walked through to oncology for Mum to have blood taken, the results of which wouldn't be known until later that afternoon.

We took up our position in Dr John's waiting room, the quiet one where everyone talked in hushed tones. It occurred to me that at none of these doctor's appointments had we ever seen anyone that looked like they were at death's door. There were obvious signs of people who had received treatment, bright beanies and scarves that covered the telltale signs of chemotherapy, but no one looked gravely ill.

Dr John opened his door. 'See you next week,' he said to the woman leaving his room. He turned his attention to the three of us, sitting like ducks in a row, waiting to be called. 'Pamela,' he said with a gentle smile and gestured for us to enter.

I introduced Mary-Ann, and Dr John took his place behind his large desk. Without fuss or fanfare he gave us the news we had come to hear. 'I've spoken to several people. I even called the one offering the best chance a second time, but I was knocked back. Pam isn't a possible candidate for any liver trials at the moment.'

Whilst the news he had just delivered wasn't a total shock I could feel my heart start to beat faster and I started to grasp at straws. 'You said "at the moment". Is that because her ammonia levels are still too high? Won't the blood results today tell us if they have dropped? Could that change things?'

'No, no one will be taking her,' he replied.

'Doctor, what if I can use my own contacts to see if I can get her on a trial?'

'If you know someone that can help you, go for it by all means.'

I knew that as soon as our meeting was over I would ring anyone and everyone who might be able to help Mum to be considered for a trial. Perhaps in making my mental checklist I missed the doctor's poignant pause.

'I'm afraid there is nothing left to try.'

I loudly exhaled the deep breath I hadn't even realised I was holding. I looked to Mum, who had in an instinctive, protective action reached out to squeeze my hand, and with a soft smile, sad eyes and clear voice, she broke the silence.

'Well, we gave it a good go didn't we?'

I sat there holding Mum's left hand; Mary-Ann was holding her right, squeezing it tightly. In what seemed like an instant my mother looked different, like she was dying.

The knockout blow had been delivered and nothing was going to change the outcome, but I still wanted to know why Mum's decline had been so rapid. Had the virus she caught in hospital robbed us of precious weeks or in fact months?

'It's hard to say, but I think it has made a difference of a few weeks not months.'

Dr John moved the conversation to how the last few weeks of Mum's life were likely to play out, and began to outline the palliative-care options available. As if switching into a different gear, Mum interrupted him mid sentence and with strength and absolute clarity stated what she wanted.

'I want to die at home and I want it to be quick.'

In a careful and considered way the experienced oncologist gave his response. 'I'm sorry, I can't do home visits, you would need to be in hospital.'

There was silence. It was a choice neither of us had anticipated having to make. I knew Mum really liked and trusted Dr John and was confident he would do what he could to ensure the process didn't drag, but it meant she would have to die in hospital.

'You don't have to decide today, Pam.'

But Mum already knew what was more important to her.

'I want to die at home.'

With care and patience Dr John talked us through how Mum's body would begin to shut down and how her pain could be managed, despite her being allergic to morphine. Apart from nausea, fatigue and a few aches I had never noticed Mum to be in any real pain. I didn't know whether that was a sign of good pain management by her doctors or whether she was good at disguising it, possibly a combination of both. We went through the list of medications she was on, some she could stop taking immediately, others she would continue. The only drug that I had remembered the name of was dexamethasone because it was the one that carried our hopes of Mum being accepted onto a liver trial. I mentioned that the nurses from palliative care had suggested there was no need for Mum to take it anymore. Dr John was very careful in his response. 'Pam, the dexamethasone is making the ammonia levels high and stripping the muscles but it is also prolonging your life.'

In a reflex reaction I couldn't help but see an opportunity, a sliver of hope. 'So can't we increase the dose of the dexamethasone and give Mum more time?'

Dr John quickly thwarted my rationale. 'No, it doesn't work quite like that. It gives more time as in days, maybe weeks, not months. Just know that when you drop the levels of dexamethasone everything will happen quickly, within forty-eight hours.'

His words shocked me. Forty-eight hours? I wasn't expecting it to be that quick. I needed Mum to fully comprehend what would happen when the dexamethasone was withdrawn. I wanted her to realise that I was not willing to make the call of when she would stop taking it.

'Mum, do you understand what will happen when you stop taking the dexamethasone?'

She nodded.

'You realise that you have to decide when you want to stop taking it, not me?'

'Yes.'

Dr John then got up from his desk. 'I want you to know that the specialist you saw first for treatment did everything right. Nothing would really have changed this outcome.'

With that, Mum looked at her oncologist and gave him a small but genuine smile. 'Thank you, John.'

She turned to me, drew in a large breath. 'OK! Let's go home and get on with it.'

It was clear there would be no more appointments and no more treatments unless by some miracle I could find a way to get her on a liver trial.

Over the past year whilst sitting in medical waiting rooms I had often wondered how doctors and specialists who deal with dying people actually say goodbye when they know it's the last time they are likely to see a patient. Do they in fact say goodbye? I was intrigued as to how it would all be wrapped up; I was about to find out.

It was like waiting for the fat lady to sing, waiting for the last words he would say to us, not that I was really expecting anything poignant or profound, I just wanted to know what the actual words would be.

Dr John opened the door for us and, as I pushed the wheelchair through, Mum looked up at him and smiled.

'See ya later, Pam,' he said. That was it! I almost wanted to laugh but I didn't. Oh the irony of anticlimax.

The next patient's name was called and we made our way to the reception desk to settle the account. The lady was kind but didn't ask if we needed another appointment. We made our way down the very quiet corridor.

'Sorry but I need the bathroom,' Mum said. It was a simple request but it felt ill-timed given the blow we had just been delivered. Then again, 'real life' may have been just the diversion we needed, and the three of us still managed a laugh at our lack of nursing skills. We were clueless as to what position to put the wheelchair in once we all made it inside the cubicle, or how to lift Mum from the wheelchair to the toilet seat, and the seemingly simple task turned into a ridiculous marathon.

The sky was dark and it was raining when we drove from the hospital, the weather mirroring how I felt. Nothing much was being said, though many questions ran through my mind. Was she scared? Had she given up? Was she really ready to die? Was she too sick and tired to care? I could see she was depleted of all energy, as was I, and I knew the time wasn't right to ask.

The traffic moved slowly and I watched the windscreen wipers move back and forth, taking in more of the surrounds than I usually would. We drove past the city landmarks, the Melbourne Cricket Ground, the Botanic Gardens, where people were going about their everyday. I was catching quick glimpses of Mum looking out the window. As we drove along Punt Road, it dawned on me that this was the last time she would ever see the familiar streets she would have driven down hundreds of times during her life. Was she taking it in like I was? Or was it nothing more than a blank stare? It was another question I kept to myself. The next fifteen minutes marked her final look at the outside world, another 'last'. There had already been lots of 'lasts':

the final time we went out for lunch, the last afternoon she spent in her garden, we just didn't realise at the time that they were in fact 'lasts'.

The rain began to fall harder for just a few moments before stopping quite suddenly. Like big teardrops, I thought to myself, simultaneously cringing at the corny movie-type cliché playing in my head. Mum loved the rain; perhaps that wasn't the last time she would see it, it was winter after all, but I made a mental note anyway in case it was. It was almost certainly the last time she would ride in a car or stop at traffic lights. She was going home to die. We knew that once inside the house she was never coming out again, not alive anyway.

It was a calm silence. There was no sense of anticipation, no sign of anger or disappointment. When required, Mum was very good at keeping up appearances or putting on a brave face but I could tell when there was pretence and in that moment there was none. It was an air of acceptance. Mum could say hand on heart that she'd given it her best shot, made good on a promise to her children, but fate had dealt its hand.

I've never been good at accepting things I cannot change – in fact I think I have spent a disproportionate amount of time getting all worked up about them to no avail. Mum's approach was far more philosophical.

'It is what it is!' And ranting and raving about what was coming wouldn't do anyone any good.

In the home stretch, we drove past the children's school. Mum was still gazing out the window as we passed by the deserted playground and the milkbar where she would take the kids to buy ice cream after school. I pressed the control that would activate the garage door as we turned into the street, and as I drove into the garage the door came down on Mum's outside world.

I helped her undress and get into bed. As I carried the clothes to the laundry and placed them in the basket I realised she would never do another load of washing or even get dressed again. The black winter coat I'd bought for her birthday just four weeks before was hanging in the wardrobe. We both knew she had chosen the bigger size so that I could use it, but had she expected to be handing it over so soon? I cast my eyes over the row of clothes hanging on sturdy white plastic hangers; she didn't like the thin wire ones. All her lovely clothes: a few designer pieces she had paid a fortune for, others she had bought at the high-end recycled-clothing boutique. Mum was great at mixing high end with low and loved a bargain. If she found a good buy she would usually purchase it in several colours. 'Going broke saving money again,' she would joke.

I placed her black loafers back at the bottom of the wardrobe alongside her many other pairs, so many different shades and styles. As she had got older the heels had become a little lower and more sensible for everyday wear but she still had plenty of high heels. 'I need the height,' she would insist, even if it did play hell with her bunion. I was casting my eye up and down the shoe rack when a bright pink pair caught my eye and triggered a funny memory. The court shoe with a two-inch block heel was covered in hot-pink material with multiple small metal squares on the toe and back. When she'd shown me, I'd joked, 'Well, we certainly won't lose you in those. What are you planning to wear them with?' As if pulling a rabbit out of a hat she declared, 'With this!' and unwrapped a hot-pink knee-length pencil skirt with a matching winged coat she had bought; there was even a bag to match.

Mum had the confidence to add that bit of edge with the unusual shoes and pulled it off beautifully. It was a stunning ensemble and never failed to draw compliments. My happy memory disintegrated as I caught myself marking off another 'last'. She would never wear those pink shoes again – in fact, none of the shoes would ever go on her feet again. Unfortunately they wouldn't go on mine either, they were all too small, two sizes too small. Despite the sound of the death knell ringing loudly I knew I had to press on and snapped myself out of the sad thoughts that were lingering, threatening to break me. I closed the wardrobe doors and returned to Mum's side.

'You need to eat something. There's still some brains in the fridge.' Just saying the words 'brains' made me want to gag, but she loved them and one of her other sisters had cooked some and dropped them over.

'No, I'm not hungry,' Mum said.

I wondered if her lost appetite was due to the physical effects of the cancer and the medications or if it was an emotional reaction. She may have been expecting Dr John to say there was nothing more that could be done, but to actually hear the words was a fair amount to digest. No wonder she didn't want to eat, no one did. The morning outing had clearly taken its toll and I left her to sleep.

Out of habit I walked to the kitchen and pressed the button down on the kettle. Mary-Ann and I stood in silence as we listened to the surge of power as the water began to heat. The crescendo of loud bubbles signalled boiling point and there was the click of the automatic off switch before the silence returned.

'Do you want tea, Mare?'

'No thanks, Kel.'

'Me neither.'

The metaphorical sand of my mother's life was rapidly running out, and I found myself swinging between rationally organising and prioritising things that needed to be done with her affairs and madly grasping at slim hopes that might give her one last reprieve.

I picked up the phone and rang a colleague, a medical journalist who had some serious heavyweight contacts. She knew that Mum was sick and over the past year I had run the names of Mum's doctors and professional opinions past her, though I had never asked for any favours or strings to be pulled. I scolded myself. Why hadn't I done this earlier? I felt foolish for following protocol – it wasn't going to save my mother.

'Could you see if there are any trials Mum might be considered for?' Even as I asked the question I knew it was too late; my colleague needed time and that was something we simply didn't have much of. I didn't tell Mum about the conversation, but couldn't help indulging in a fantasy of a last-minute intervention. I wasn't hoping for a miracle cure, just some more time.

She wore Berry Couture

The soft sunlight coming from the sewing room caught my eye. Mum's sewing machine was still set up on the glass table against the window, the scissors right where she had left them. The giant bead box was open and contained thousands of little sparkles in all shapes and sizes that she would handpick and cluster together, trusted glue gun at the ready.

Seeing the battered old glue gun made me smile. It was old and had blobs of paint caked onto it, but it had served her well. It was one of her most trusted tools in her florist shop and was still getting plenty of use in her new career as seamstress Nana.

'Why would I spend hours sewing on beads and bling when I can glue them in two seconds?' she would say. Burning a finger was par for the course when using it but Mum just got accustomed to yelling 'Ouch'. She'd suck her finger to ease the pain then continue.

Should've! Could've! Would've! Didn't! I scolded myself, lamenting missed opportunities to spend more time with Mum, learning to sew. We had started off well with the sacks but there had always been something to distract me and I had already forgotten what Mum had taught me. I liked the romance of continuing a tradition she'd started but didn't apply myself to master the task. It didn't matter really, Mum had already sewn more Santa sacks than there were ever likely to be grandchildren, but she wanted to be certain that every one of them had something from the Nana they would never know. I had clear instructions on where to send the calico label for the name to be embroidered and there was a stash of Christmas ornaments for me to glue on depending on whether the child was a girl or boy.

How had I miscalculated the time Mum had left? I wondered, and clearly I wasn't the only one caught out. Looking at the half-sewn pieces placed to the side and snippets of cotton threads that were still on the floor, Mum had obviously thought she had more time too. The room looked as though she had just left to make a cup of tea.

Palliative care arrived mid afternoon. I updated the nurse on our appointment with the doctor, and in a self-deprecating way, explained how difficult it had become to physically move Mum by relaying the bathroom episode.

'Why don't we insert a catheter?' she suggested. 'It will take the pressure off you.'

My initial thought was to refuse. I didn't mind helping Mum, it didn't bother me in the slightest, the pressure on me didn't need to be relieved, and I wanted to keep my mother's dignity.

'You know a catheter will also mean your mother can conserve her energy. Just getting to the toilet now is exhausting for her. Why don't we pop one in and if she improves or she finds it uncomfortable we can take it out. We'll show you how to use hot towels to bathe her, patients find it very soothing.'

'What do you think, Mum?'

'It's probably a good idea,' she said in a conciliatory tone.

The benefits of the catheter were hard to ignore but it felt like another nail in the proverbial coffin. Just a few hours earlier we had to accept that she would never leave the house again. Now it seemed she would never even leave her room.

After the nurse left I sat on the side of Mum's bed and released a deflated sigh, inviting a moment to recognise the latest step in her decline, but I should've known better than to think Mum would indulge in self-pity.

'Are you all right?' she asked, and reached for my hand.

'I'm supposed to be asking if you are all right, not the other way round. Here, have a jellybean, let's get your ammonia levels down.' She rolled her eyes. 'Do it for me. I've made some calls to see if there are any other trials you might be able to get on. Do you want a cup of tea?'

'No, no tea. Are the boys coming tonight?'

'Yes, they'll be here after work.'

Just a few minutes later she was sleeping again.

I sat there a little longer and my eyes wandered into her ensuite, noting that the contents of the catheter would need to be emptied there. I'd better make sure it's clean, I thought. Mum would die if anyone went in there and it wasn't spotless.

As I squirted disinfectant in the toilet and replaced the towels, I noticed her jars of creams lined up on the bench. She had used them religiously morning and night her entire life for her dry skin; she would never use them again. There were boxes of pills that would not be finished, the shampoo in the shower. I was mentally cataloguing all of it, even the half-used bar of soap. 'Stop!' I muttered to myself. Who takes notice of a half-used bar of soap?

I opened the drawer under the sink that I knew would contain Mum's lipsticks. I shook my head in amusement that her love of lipstick had endured. There must have been twenty of them. Some containers were black, others were gold, but all were Revlon. The cosmetic brushes she had used to apply her make-up that morning still lay on the bathroom bench, and I became lost in a moment that seemed to last a very long time. The eyeshadow palette of brown and crème hues was well used; the eyeliner needed sharpening, the blush was clearly a new purchase as it had no signs of wear. I couldn't bring myself to put them into their rightful place, as if to do so would somehow be erasing a 'last'.

I knew that if I shared my sentimental thought with Mum she would say, 'Don't be ridiculous! How long are you going to leave them there for?' I ignored her imagined voice of reason and left them in situ. Everything was frozen in time. Mum was still alive though her living was now complete; she had upheld her part of the agreement to give the fight against cancer her best shot and it was time for me to deliver on mine. It was time for dying; there was much to do.

'Let's make a list!' I suggested as I propped the big white pillow behind Mum's back so that she was sitting up.

'What sort of list?'

'A shopping list?' I said, voice dripping with sarcasm. 'I think we should make a list of the people you want to see.'

There was no need to say 'for the last time', no need to state the obvious. I knew it had already been an emotionally and physically draining day but she was better for sleeping most of the afternoon and I didn't want to waste precious time. I sat with pen poised and a few seconds passed before she responded in a very neutral tone: 'I don't want to see anyone.'

It wasn't that I expected names of long-lost friends or those she hadn't seen in a while, but I assumed that once she knew the final curtain was about to come down there would be a few close friends and family that she would want to see.

'Don't be ridiculous,' I said curtly. 'This isn't just about you.' Whilst Mary-Ann was coming every day, Mum had two other sisters and a brother and they needed to be able to say goodbye.

Mum took in a deep breath and exhaled. 'OK.'

I began writing their names on the notepad. 'Surely there must be some others you want to see.'

There was another pause. 'Pat.'

Aunty Pat was my father's big sister. I knew she and Mum had a lovely relationship but I would never have guessed she would be the only name Mum would ask to have on her list.

As I wrote her name down I asked, 'Why Pat?'

'Before all of you came along your father and I spent a lot of time with Pat and Jack and their kids. She was very good to me, all those years when I was waiting for your father to marry me and long after. Most of our weekends would be spent at their house.'

'OK, I'll ring her. Do you want me to ring Susie?'

'No, don't ring Suse, she won't come.'

I didn't believe her for a second. Susie had been her best friend for sixty-five years. She lived interstate but I knew she would travel any distance to be there for Mum.

'Rubbish! I'm going to call her anyway.'

I rattled off a few other names in case she needed prompting but the answer was the same: 'No.'

I took Mum's brown address book from the bedside table and left to make the calls. I rang Susie and filled her in on Mum's rapid decline.

'Thank you, but I won't come,' she said. 'We have already said our goodbyes.'

Just a few weeks earlier Susie had made the trip down from her home in Australia's capital to spend a weekend at the beach with the woman she had shared a lifetime of friendship with. They weren't going to wait for the mad scramble; they both knew it was the last time they would see each other. That dignified foresight lent itself to what I imagined was not an over-the-top long torturous goodbye but a simple and loving conclusion. Drama never had been their thing.

How did that mother of mine get so wise? She had already seen the people she wanted to see. She knew visitors took energy and that there was little point in wearing herself out. What could anyone say? She wanted to conserve what was left for the ones she loved most, her children. Nothing else mattered.

The phone was still in my hand when it rang. It was Dr John with the results of the blood tests taken that morning, even though it felt like days ago.

'The cancer markers have dropped significantly and your mother's ammonia levels have dropped by a third.'

My heart skipped a beat. Were those damn jellybeans I had been popping into her mouth every time she looked at me actually doing something to reduce her ammonia levels? It was the ammonia levels that needed to drop to allow her even to be considered for a trial. Perhaps it wasn't too late.

When I relayed the results to Mum and then my brothers that evening we couldn't help but feel buoyed. It was a small turnaround but it was something, and the day certainly ended with better news than when it had begun. We stood around in Mum's room and the brothers and I filled our glasses with red wine.

'Here's to the jellybeans,' I laughed and raised my glass.

'You're kidding aren't you?' snapped Robert. 'It's not the jellybeans, it's the jungle juice.'

The new day unfolded in a similar sequence to those of the previous week; one of my brothers stayed the night and I arrived after school to take over.

My first job was to give Mum her tablets. In an effort to avoid any confusion and danger of missing out on medication or doubling up I was the official 'pill police', administering around twenty-five tablets a day. A printed sheet would tell me the name, how many and how often. I sat on Mum's bed and counted them out. 'Two of that one, three of that one …' It was easy to get confused. During the dispensary session that morning Mum watched me.

'You're missing one,' she said.

'No I'm not.'

'Yes you are. You're missing a white one.'

'Oh, you fool! I am not!' I got up off the bed in an effort to not only appease her but also prove her wrong. A single white pill dropped to the floor. Nothing was said but Mum's raised eyebrows and Cheshire Cat smile spoke volumes. 'Mother knows best.'

An afternoon visit from palliative care gave us reassurance that Mum was comfortable but once again the nurse urged me to reduce the level of the dexamethasone. Again I explained that I wasn't the one to make that decision and deferred to Mum.

'Do you want to continue taking the dexamethasone?'

'Yes, I'll keep taking it.'

Phew, I thought, feeling instant relief. Her response surprised me somewhat given that there were no treatments left for her to try, and whilst I knew I had no right to ask her to keep taking the medication I sure as hell wasn't about to argue if she wanted to.

The nurse respected Mum's decision and replied with a non-judgemental and neutral 'OK', leaving the dexamethasone on the medical chart.

I was so grateful that Mum was still able to articulate her wishes; she simply wasn't ready for the consequences of reducing the drug, though I never even asked her why. Frankly I didn't care, but it was clear she was in complete control. I would have hated to have to guess what Mum actually wanted. It must be agonising for people who have to make such hard decisions when their loved one can't verbalise theirs.

The inevitable was fast approaching and even though I knew it was a long shot that any cancer trial program would accept Mum the equation in my mind was simple: dexamethasone plus reduced ammonia levels equalled 'more time'. Time was what I needed for Mum to make decisions on important matters relating to her funeral and to make sure her will was in order. There were also other matters I wanted addressed: was she sure she wanted me to have her jewellery? What did she want done with her furniture and car? How did I take care of her beautiful orchid? From a purely selfish point of view, as long as Mum wasn't in pain and could still talk to me I wanted to grab every bonus hour we could get to be together, but I knew we needed to use it wisely. It was precious time to prepare all of us to accept that our mother's death was imminent.

There was a gentle silence in the room as the nurse finished up her checks, but it was broken by a simple suggestion that burst one of my last bubbles of hope.

'You need to stop giving your mother the jellybeans, it's counterproductive for her blood pressure.'

'OK,' I said, feeling as if someone had just handed me two buckets of lead. I attempted to justify my actions and perhaps sway the nurse's opinion. 'It's just that we are trying to keep her ammonia low. We found out yesterday that the cancer markers have dropped, you know.'

The nurse's smile was kind and her tone was caring. 'I'm afraid the latest markers are no disguise for the failing body.'

My thoughts of jellybeans vanished. 'How soon are we talking? A week? A few days?'

'It's hard to know, but I would say days,' the nurse estimated.

My shoulders slumped with the weight of her expert opinion, the word 'days' echoing in my head. My thoughts raced ahead. This time next week she will be dead. This time next week she won't be here. There was now no hope of us going away for our special few days together. We were entering the last few days of my mother's life. My heart began to race. 'Days' was a number between one and seven, which would it be? There was a huge difference. I turned to my aunt, who looked sad and drawn. She had just made arrangements for her siblings to visit Mum over the next seven days. 'Mare, you need to phone everyone and bring the visits forward, we're running out of time.'

Mum was the oldest of five; the age difference between her and the youngest spanned almost fifteen years. She was not really like any of them to look at it, and over the years there had been talk both as a joke and a serious aside that perhaps they didn't all share the same father. The long absences of the war years gave weight to the theory, yet it had never really bothered Mum whether the man she called 'Dad' was her biological father or not.

Throughout my life Mum's three sisters and brother and their families had been at all major family events and milestones. Distance played a big part in how much we saw them but so did sheer difference. Different personalities, different stages of life and different social circles had created the ebbs and flows of sibling interaction. However, distance and differences dissolved as soon as they received the call to come quickly, the family ties that bound them pulled and held tight.

As each of them arrived at the house I wondered how those final days would play out for all of them. Their big sister 'Pammie' had been there for them. Whether it was conscious or not, for some she had become a surrogate mother figure when theirs had died.

One of her sisters had dropped in several times over the past few days with food; she'd speak to Mum for a few minutes and then leave. They had never been very close, siblings aren't necessarily friends, but her hand was raised high to offer any help that was needed. I don't know if they ever exchanged words to resolve any issues but my heart was heavy. It wouldn't matter for Mum, she would be dead; it's the ones left behind who are burdened with regrets: 'What if' and 'If only'. All that seemed to matter, though, was that in those final days there was love and kindness.

Each of them spent several short bursts with Mum and in between I enjoyed cups of tea with them in the kitchen, chatting and swapping information on the progress of the family's newest generation, the great-nieces and -nephews.

She wore Blasé Apricot

My mother kept all of our childhood health records, small grey paper booklets that documented birth weight, weekly weight gain, and immunisations. She had also kept a lock of hair from each child's first haircut and our first few baby teeth in sealed envelopes. I thought this was adequate until my friends and I started having children and discovered that their mothers had kept newborn outfits, baby singlets, first shoes, first dresses, cots and baby blankets. I felt cheated that I had nothing from my infancy to hand down to my child.

'Why didn't you keep anything of mine, Mum?'

She was unapologetic. 'What would I want to keep baby singlets for? I threw them out. We had no room to store a cot for thirty-five years. Don't be ridiculous.'

'You're not very sentimental,' I said, sulking.

'About used baby singlets? No.' She laughed. 'I don't even know what happened to my wedding dress actually, let alone baby singlets.'

If ever I needed information on my childhood, whether it was milestones, episodes of illness or other significant events, all I had to do was ask Mum, she remembered most of it. And although the passing years eroded her ability to recall many of the details, she would simply conclude, 'It can't have been that important.'

When I became a mother, almost everyone I spoke to wanted to share words of wisdom and advice. Among the plethora of conflicting suggestions was: 'Write the special moments down because you will forget.' I remember making a mental note to make sure I recorded the date of every 'first'. Determined to keep better records and details for my children than my mother did for me, the first thing I kept was a week-by-week video of the growing bump. I had a little box containing the scans, the birth notice from the newspaper announcing McKenzie's arrival into the world and the hospital identity band. A lock of hair was preserved, as was the newborn outfit our daughter arrived home from hospital in. In a special book I diligently recorded that date of her first smile, first tooth, the first time she rolled over, her first word, first crawl, first food and first step. I don't remember when my efforts began to dissipate but a funny thing called 'life' got in the way and I stopped. I didn't consciously cease making entries but the end result was the same. With each new baby I pledged to do at least the equivalent to what I had done for our first baby but didn't, and by the time our fourth and final child James came along, he came home from hospital in the same outfit that his three sisters had worn and was lucky to get much more than his name and weight written down. Even then we didn't use his name for years, we just called him 'Boy'. I am confident I can recall important details for each of them and many amusing encounters, though sometimes for the life of me I can't remember which child they relate to.

I have to admit that for all that I do remember, there is plenty more that I don't, memories now lost forever. Every now and then when mother guilt bites me, especially when one of my children begs me to recall something specific and unique to them from their toddler years, I heed the advice given by a friend whose wise words were simply to 'make it up. Kids don't know and don't care if they're true; they just want a story with their name in it'.

I still toggle between making a tangible record of life events and simply enjoying a moment and letting it go.

Trying to freezeframe it on various devices means I am living through a camera lens and potentially missing much more. And to what end anyway? I have taken hours of home video footage of 'priceless' unrepeatable moments, none of which I have ever watched and wonder whether I ever will.

Mum looked small and frail amongst the big white pillows that surrounded her as she lay sleeping. Her skin had developed a yellow tinge and the definition of her high cheekbones had all but vanished beneath the puffiness caused by her medication, but her breathing was calm and she seemed peaceful.

It struck me that I was not only about to lose her from my daily life but that I was also losing our family's personal reference library. The big things such as major life events or significant happenings would likely be recalled by a close relative or family friend but it was the small pieces of interesting history that would be lost. Like the annoying little odd pieces of a jigsaw that one can never seem to find.

I knew that I could ask and she would tell me. In my early childhood and young-adult years the answers may have been age appropriate but since becoming a mother, now that I was a member of the same club, her answers would be completely honest, warts and all. But it wasn't enough for her to just tell me, I needed to write it down because with so much going on I was likely to forget.

Whilst Mum continued to sleep I grabbed my notebook and began writing down a list of questions that I thought might one day pop into my head. Questions I would wish I had asked, or maybe I had asked and already forgotten the answers to. What was her first job? Who was her first boyfriend? Where did her white fox fur come from? Did any of her many pieces of jewellery have any special significance? She had been a talented ballet dancer but I never really knew why she gave it up. She had been engaged twice before she married Dad; who were they and why did they break up? What made her closer to some siblings than others? What were the Lotto numbers she had been taking for years? There was no sequence to my questions and none would be off bounds, the last few days would be my last opportunity.

Whilst there were many things I wanted to know, the more pressing issue was my list of things to do. I turned to the back of the A4 folder where I had compiled another list of questions that needed answers.

I was still sitting watching Mum and writing when she woke. As she opened her eyes she looked around the room, then caught my eye and smiled.

'How are you feeling?'

'I'm OK.'

'Good. I have some questions for you. What hymns and songs do you want played?'

I sensed indifference in her reply. 'I don't mind, you choose.'

There were songs embedded in my memory, songs that over the years she had flippantly said, 'Make sure you play this at my funeral.'

'So how about "Wind Beneath My Wings"?'

'Oh, God, no!' she spat. 'No, not that.' It had been twenty-odd years since the Bette Midler hit was on high rotation on radio and clearly Mum had moved on. All I could be thankful for was thinking to mention it, because if I hadn't asked there was nothing more certain than that the *Beaches* movie tearjerker would have been on the front line of the funeral playlist.

It was apparent that I couldn't leave anything to chance or memory. I was going to double-check every dying wish of my mother, every single one I thought I knew, which clearly I didn't, or that I did and she had decided to change.

For all my mother's style and effortless flair I knew one of the most bizarre questions I needed to ask was, 'What do you want to wear in the coffin?' Some may find that crass. Was it necessary? Absolutely. Why? Because otherwise the decision would have been left with me. I knew I would have stressed over what outfit to choose. I wanted to take the guesswork out of it. I'm glad I did.

'I want to wear my white nightie,' she said. I thought I knew my mother inside and out but never ever would have I expected her to say that.

'Are you serious?'

She was.

It's not that I was planning to doll her up in her best dress or go over the top, but a nightgown? Her reason was simple. 'There's no point! It's going up in smoke anyway, I'd rather leave my nice things for you to wear.'

The nightdress she was referring to had been a gift for her birthday; it was simple, pretty and white. Mum loved white, bleach white. If she had a fetish for anything it was bleach, she used it everywhere. It was used in the flower water of her shop because it made them last longer, to clean floors, jewellery and of course clothes. Goodness knows how many items of clothing were ruined over our lifetime by the stray splash of bleach, but it never deterred her. I wrote 'white nightie' on the list.

'What about make-up? No one can do it like you. I can't bear the thought of you looking like anyone other than you. How do we get around that? What colour lipstick?'

'I won't need any make-up once I'm gone, that's it. I want you to say goodbye to me at home and that is the end of it. There will be no viewing, I don't want you or anybody else standing over a coffin crying. I couldn't bear it.'

I actually hadn't given it much thought until then but I understood her reasoning. Dad's death came with very little warning. We knew that his lifestyle suggested he was on borrowed time, but when he had left for work one cold morning in June we never imagined that he wouldn't be coming back. Seeing him after he had died confirmed what was hard to believe and was a chance to say goodbye. In stark contrast, whilst Mum's terminal illness had been hanging heavily around our necks for a year, it had given us ample time to prepare, subconsciously or otherwise. Whether we missed the actual moment of death or not we would still see her just after she'd taken her last breath. There was no need to have one final look a few days later.

She wore Misty Cinnamon

I became the self-designated 'door bitch'. My job was to field calls from well-wishers and kindly but firmly deny all requests from those wanting to see or speak to Mum. I completely understood when some were taken aback, albeit only slightly, but how I admired my mother's clarity in knowing the impact it would have on the time she had left.

How wonderful were the souls who didn't take offence at not being granted an audience and instead put pen to paper. Handwritten letters arrived in the mailbox or were slipped under the front door and I would sit on the bed and read them out to Mum. I'm so thankful for those who thought to do it. Their words were warm and generous and came from people she had known for decades and others only in more recent years.

'Pam, I admired how you have put your family first …'

There were letters from nieces and nephews Mum had not seen for some time recalling happy moments shared with my mother long before I was born.

'Pammie, my thoughts are with you as you navigate this sad farewell. I have admired your courage and forthrightness to face what is before you. I remember as a child the wonderful smells of your florist shop.'

'Pammie, I have wonderful childhood memories of visiting you most Sundays with plenty of laughter and a cup of tea.'

'Pammie, you made each of us feel special.'

I was overwhelmed at their beautiful simplicity, recounting simple acts that my mother probably never gave a second thought to but which had found a permanent place in the hearts and memories of others.

Emotions and the gravity of death might in an intimate face-to-face encounter leave even the bravest lost for words, but the sentiments on paper provided snapshots of joy and appreciation where Mum could still feel comfort from those who loved her. As I read and reread each one I couldn't help but feel puzzled and sad, wondering why so many people, me included, leave the sharing of such heartfelt sentiments until after someone has passed away.

Pat came to the door with a bunch of Singapore orchids, wearing bright lipstick and a warm smile. 'Hello, Kellie,' she said in her deep rustic voice but with perfectly formed vowels. This was a lady who knew all about death. Both her parents had died when she was in her twenties and that made her an instant matriarch to four younger siblings, including my father. Pat had also lived every parent's worst nightmare, burying one of her twelve children, who had died in a car accident. It had also only been a few months earlier that Jack, her husband of more than five decades, had passed away. I don't know if her experiences made it easier or harder to visit Mum; she had pretty much seen it all.

I walked Pat into Mum's room.

'Hello, Pamela Mary, I bought you some orchids in case you wanted to whip up a posy.'

A smile spread across my face at our family's humour, dry as a chip. She sat down on the bed and held Mum's hand; the smile they shared was one of those knowing smiles, as if Mum was saying, 'It's my turn.' There was no need for me to be there; in fact, it seemed wrong for me to stay.

'I'm going to make tea,' I said and didn't return. Instead I sat in the kitchen weeping for the conversation I was not privy to and wondered what they would be saying.

Pat stayed no more than half an hour. She had a perfect sense of timing and knew when to go. I heard her quietly close Mum's door and took it as my cue to return from 'making tea'. I walked her out and thanked her for coming. I never asked Mum what they discussed.

There was an unopened envelope on the bedside table. It simply said 'Mum'. I opened it and immediately scanned to the bottom to see whom it was from. 'Mum, it's a letter from Robert.' My older brother had called in first thing that morning to see Mum before he left to do a job interstate. He hadn't told anyone he'd left a letter. 'Mum I think you need to read this one,' I said, holding out the letter to her.

She didn't extend her hand. 'Read it to me.'

I felt decidedly uncomfortable about her request. Rob was never one for expressing himself and if he'd gone to the trouble to write a letter I knew it wouldn't be intended for my eyes. 'I don't feel like I should be reading this, Mum.'

'I can't,' she replied, and I realised she physically couldn't. 'I need you to read it for me.'

I sat next to her on the side of the bed feeling like an intruder listening to the intimate thoughts of a son to his mother.

'This will be the hardest love letter I ever write. It's also probably the longest letter I have ever written to you, so my timing sucks!'

My mute tears started flowing almost immediately as the penned words of the firstborn expressed what he couldn't verbalise because he found it too difficult. On paper he perfectly articulated his love and gratitude to Mum for being the ultimate teacher and for believing in her children. 'Forever the eternal optimist, nothing gets in your way. You're a doer, a lady of action, the world's greatest mother and we are so proud of you in every way. It's our turn to look after you and we love it so don't feel for one second you have to go before you're ready. I love you so much and find it hard to believe there will be a time when you won't answer my call. Mum, I will always be very very grateful.'

My full-blown waterworks continued until the very last word. I looked at Mum and feared she would be faring worse than me but she wasn't. She smiled a semi-smile that showed a mother's pride, but her deep breath in and slow release revealed what I guessed was a mother's feeling of utter helplessness when she is unable to ease her child's sorrow and pain.

She wore Butterfly Pink

They say it takes a village to raise a child, but it is the women of the village who are truly amazing, and the sisterhood never ceases to amaze me.

Without fanfare or fuss they come together like worker bees for another sister in need. A group can be made up of close friends, old friends, acquaintances or simply the mother of your child's friend. As one of the many who at different times has done a small part to help someone in need, I had never given it much thought, it was no big deal; but to be on the receiving end of such kindness was truly remarkable.

I'm not one to readily accept help from others, I like to try and do it all, to think of myself as 'capable'. It took the caring but firm words of a friend who said 'Just let us help you' to finally hand over my silly pride.

Women wanted to help in any way they could and in any way I needed, helping to ease my load and freeing me to spend more time caring for Mum. When I gave the green light the village swung into action. Women didn't bombard me with questions about what I needed because the sisterhood knows that sometimes just thinking about what you need takes more effort than actually doing it yourself. I was kept informed by either email or SMS about who was doing what.

'I'm picking up the kids from school today and will be taking them to the park for an hour.'

'I will take Stella to my house for the day.'

'I will collect and drop Sidney.'

Meals just appeared in the fridge with sticky notes attached: 'Beef lasagne – can go in the freezer if you have lasagne overload.' People were at the ready to do anything to help, even delousing one of my children.

Ah yes, lice, those disgusting crawly creatures, have no regard for timing. The thought of having to spend an hour combing through my daughter's hair looking for a suspected infestation of nits and eggs filled me with dread on any given day, let alone when my mother was dying. The sign of a true friend is when you can call them and ask them to check your child's itchy head and without hesitation hear the reply, 'Of course.'

The beautiful thing about women of the village is that practical help is provided with no strings attached. Their motivation is nothing other than to help another sister in need, and so many times when I would thank them profusely the standard reply was, 'You would do the same for me.' It reminded me of how my mother had always operated. I don't think she ever came to my home and sat on a couch waiting to be served a cup of tea or anything else for that matter. We might have sat on the couch together folding washing, or talked whilst I chopped vegetables and she peeled potatoes. When I had a newborn baby she would sit for a cuddle but then would be up sweeping my floor or putting washing on the line. 'What do you need doing?' she would ask. 'Give me a job!'

The women who helped out knew I had little time to chat or for cups of tea. Even when my manners got the better of me and I invited them in they refused. But on one of those nights whilst my brother Mick was spending time with Mum I found myself home alone. My husband Michael was out, the children were fast asleep and all of a sudden I felt lost. So much had been going on in the past few days with not a minute to spare and then out of the blue I was faced with a few hours of nothing. I didn't want to be alone.

Within an hour of sending SMS messages a few village women were quietly letting themselves in the front door that I had left ajar; women know not to ring doorbells when children are sleeping. They arrived armed with wine, chocolate and good humour. Of course their first question was, 'How's your Mum?' I was happy if not relieved to be able to debrief a little, especially as Mum's decline in recent days had been so rapid. They sat on the couch and on the floor and the conversation naturally moved onto general friendly banter. It only took a few drinks before one of the girls said, 'Well, I know this is probably inappropriate to say, but hell you look skinny. You look hot in those jeans.'

'You can't say that!' said someone else, laughing, but we all laughed loudly at the political incorrectness. A few hours' light relief was just what I had needed, especially when I knew that the next few days would bring darkness I had never known.

During those days I was also gifted something extraordinary by one of my cousins. We weren't close as young kids but one afternoon at a family function in our late teens we clicked. Our wonderful connection and shared humour didn't translate to us being good housemates, but we remained close even though she moved states twenty years ago.

I was frequently talking to her on the phone, updating her on Mum's condition, when one night she said, 'I'm going to come down for a few days to help you.'

I swiftly responded. 'Please don't, there's nothing you can do and I'm so busy that I won't have any time to spend with you.'

'I'm coming anyway,' she insisted, and jumped on a plane, leaving her son and husband at home for four days to be with me. My cousin was anything but a guest. She wasn't there to hold my hand; she moved in to provide hands-on help. My house was cleaned, washing done. She was there for the pick-up and drop-off of children; she fed them, bathed them and did anything else that needed doing in the lives of my young family. With her efforts, everything kept ticking over and the children loved her playful nature and enjoyed her undivided attention and bedtime stories. I could spend more time with Mum without worrying about what was going on at home. 'She's a good stick,' said Mum.

The night before my cousin returned home we were sharing a drink when she asked what so many others had: 'Do you think I could go and see your Mum just for a few minutes?' I could hear the hesitation in her voice as she made the request, and for all her selfless actions during that week, it seemed the very least I could do. But Mum had been so very clear: 'No one!'

In the kindest way I could, which really just meant dressing up a 'no', I explained Mum's wishes. I felt thoroughly mean. My cousin had gone way beyond the call of friendship or family, but to make an exception would potentially open the floodgates. 'I'm so sorry, you have been amazing and Mum knows how much you have been there for me this week, but if I say yes to you …'

I knew she was disappointed and yet she floored me with her good grace and understanding. 'No, I understand,' she said. 'I was just thinking that I won't be able to come back for the funeral, but it's fine. I really do understand.'

My heart was heavy. The funeral was an important part of the grieving process but I knew she had already taken time off work and if the predicted timeline of days Mum had left was right it simply wasn't feasible for my cousin to leave for a day or two and then come back.

'Cousin, you don't need to come back for the funeral. Mum wouldn't want you to. The funeral will be for people to pay tribute. You have paid your aunt the greatest tribute by being here for me.'

There was a figurative shadow over the fairy garden in my backyard. For years it had been a loving work in progress, the curator one adoring Nana.

A rocky terrain under a big gum tree was the home of Nana's fairy garden. Her weekly meanderings around local markets would almost certainly produce an offering for my little girls' piece of heaven.

It wasn't just the haven of my children; all their little friends would make a direct beeline through the front door and out to our special place. There was a treasure trove of fairies of all descriptions. Some were sleeping on leaves, others were in frozen poses of delight. They were joined by chubby gnomes in bright cone hats and magic horses with wings, all nestled in a miniature world of toadstools, tiny houses, and pebbles with the words 'laugh', 'love' and 'dream' on them, while a canopy of wooden stars and butterflies dropped from the branches and strings of beads were woven in and out.

New additions would demand a reshuffle and I would come home and find Mum and the children happily pottering as they pondered and rearranged the line-up. Mum liked a reshuffle whereas I'm a creature of habit; she embraced change, I tend to hang onto the comforts of what I know.

It was a fairy garden with purpose. It wasn't just to look pretty; it was to play in. The interactive approach however meant there were casualties. Among the prettiness were amputees, missing heads, eyes, arms and wings, but not one was ever discarded, they were all wanted and all had their place.

Everything always looked good with fairy dust and Nana was constantly arriving with bags of the bright stuff to sprinkle so that each day there was a little sparkle to catch your eye.

Just a few weeks ago Mum had turned up with pots of brightly coloured pansies and announced, 'The girls and I are going to do some gardening.' Squeals of delight came from all directions as the children ran to admire the vibrant flowers of yellow, pink and purple earmarked for the fairy garden. In an instant they were filing outside to get 'dirty' and gathered around in silence as Nana began showing them how to gently release the plant from the pot without breaking the tender roots. Once the lesson was over the garden was filled with screams of, 'Can you help me, Nana?' and, 'Look at mine, Nana.'

Cupping both hands around a mug of hot tea I stood at my back door staring through the large glass pane and fixed my eyes on the delicate petals of the pansies as they fluttered gently like butterfly wings. So pretty but they were seasonal flowers and would die soon. The fairy garden was quiet.

Children have a way of keeping things real, no matter the gravity of any situation. My kids were aware that their nana wasn't just sick, she was very sick, and I was spending most of my time with her. Their first questions in those 'concentrated' days were always to enquire after Mum. 'How is Nana?', 'Is she still alive?', 'What does she say?' Such concern and loving emotions intertwined with the everyday. 'Can we have a biscuit?', 'Do I have to go to bed?'

Despite our efforts to keep a sense of normality, I had noticed a shift in our eldest daughter McKenzie. Even though she had only just turned seven it was as if she understood perfectly what was about to happen and as I put her to bed she began to cry.

'When will I see Nana again?'

'I will take you to see her on the weekend, darling.'

'But what if she dies before then? I don't want to wait till the weekend.'

It was already Thursday but I knew I couldn't give a guarantee Mum wouldn't die before the weekend.

'OK, how about I take you to see Nana tomorrow?'

The tears that were streaming down her perfect lightly freckle-kissed face began to ease as she explained in detail what she wanted to do before her visit.

'I want to buy Nana some roses, red roses.'

'OK, we can do that.'

'They need to be red roses and I want to buy her a fairy to take with her to heaven.'

'I'm sure we can find one of those too,' I said as I stroked her soft blonde hair.

'And I need to buy her a card …' I nodded and smiled. 'I want to buy her a goodbye card'.

Her tears began again and so did mine. I could barely swallow for the lump in my throat. My little girl knew a get-well-soon card was pointless. She knew exactly what was coming and it weighed heavily. I couldn't tell her everything would be all right because it wouldn't be – there was no upside to losing Nana. I was void of any words other than, 'It's OK to be sad, I'm sad too.' Her tears became heaving sobs and I felt helpless, I was flapping around in unknown waters. I scooped her up in my arms, carried her downstairs, placed her on the couch, and with her head in my lap continued to stroke her hair until she cried herself to sleep.

Michael poured the red wine, handed me a glass and joined us on the couch. McKenzie's soft rhythmic breathing had replaced the sobs and everything was calm once more but I was filled with dread.

'Holy shit,' I said to my husband. 'This is just the warm-up. What on earth am I going to say or do when Nana actually dies?'

In an instant his eyes welled up but he didn't speak. He shuddered and shook his head, indicating he didn't know either. We knew one thing for sure: we weren't going to delay telling them like we did when the dog died.

When Lili was put down on Christmas morning we didn't want to spoil the children's happiest day of the year, so we didn't. But when they didn't ask where she was the next day or the day after we acted like cowards and said nothing. A week had passed and we were about to go for a walk. 'Where is Lili?' asked Stella. All eyes were suddenly on us and we came clean. The news of Lili's death made them sad but what really upset them was our failure to disclose the information sooner. 'Why didn't you tell us?' Long after they stopped talking about the dog, they continued to recall how they were left out of the loop on such an important issue.

I knew I was out of my depth. 'I think we should seek some professional guidance on how to best handle the kids on Mum dying, we're only going to get one shot at getting this right and I don't want to scar them by exposing them to too much or too little.'

Michael agreed. 'Who are you going to call?'

I shrugged my shoulders but at the same time knew whom I would turn to. 'Mary-Ann will know someone, maybe she can ask her school counsellor for some tips, and one of the girls I went to school with is a child psychologist, she might be able to help too.'

In the most basic form we had spent much of the past six months trying to prepare my children for their nana's imminent death. 'Nana's body is sick, the doctors are giving her medicine so that she can still have tea parties and take you for treat days.' When the kids would ask if Nana was going to die I would trot out the line on death that my mother had given to me when I was young. 'No one lives forever. Everything that lives must die one day, it's the circle of life.'

They had quickly and easily adapted to life with a sick Nana, but it had changed little of their routine or daily life. Most days Mum was still seeing them, and the wig had actually become a comic prop. Nana would arrive in the wig and during the course of the visit just about every one of them would wear it, throw it round the room or perform in it. Even sweet baby James at little more than seven months old would pull it off her head and roar with laughter. I hadn't really tried to gauge where their understanding of the whole 'death' thing was, but it became crystal clear the next morning.

It was Friday the 13th. As I lay in bed waiting for the sounds of little feet to scuttle down the hallway, I fixed my gaze on the small stained-glass windows letting in the morning light and acknowledged the irony of having made appointments for a priest and a funeral director to visit Mum on black Friday. It was unbelievable to think that just five days earlier we had still been planning to go away on our mother-daughter weekend. Had things gone to plan I would have been packing my bags and the two of us would have been leaving for the Sunshine Coast for a few days of clean organic living. Instead we were days away from her death.

My thoughts were broken by the stampede of the three girls racing for prime positions next to me in the bed. It was standard practice for Michael to rise before they did, and with a bit of luck the winner of the hallway dash would secure his empty spot whilst it was still warm. Whoever missed out on lying either side of me would be sent to James's room to retrieve their brother from his cot. He would be plonked on the bed and that is where he would stay. We would talk about many things, but in another good dose of irony that morning the subject was death.

'What happens when you die?' asked Stella.

'Well …' I said and paused. I was contemplating the most simple and honest explanation to give them.

'I know! I know!' exclaimed Sidney. It was said with such confidence that I decided to let our five-year-old enlighten her sisters with the facts about death and how it was going to play out for Nana. We were all ears.

'So!' she said, lifting her arms slightly and opening her little palms in a gesture that indicated absolute honesty and conviction. 'When you diiiiie they put you into like a guitar case and they close the lid. Then they dig a huge hole, put the guitar case in and cover it up with dirt. After that they make a sign on top that says, "Pam is in here!" Then God, who is invisible, floats you up to heaven.' Sidney was using her best twinkling fingers to indicate the seamless ascension that Nana would make into the sky.

Whilst trying not to laugh I looked at the wide-eyed expressions on the faces of McKenzie and Stella, who were both mesmerised and seemingly persuaded by their sister's version of death. A guitar case? I thought, but then figured a box was a box and that a coffin wasn't that different, and I didn't want to spoil the moment. In any case, our attention was once again on Sidney when she began to scrunch up her face, squinting her bright blue eyes open and shut.

'What are you doing?' I asked.

'I'm pinching myself so that I can cry for Nana too because everyone cries when someone dies.'

The first thing I did when I arrived at Mum's was to recount Sidney's expectations. Managing a chuckle despite her weakness she said, 'I quite like her idea of the guitar case.'

Taking her lead I chimed in, 'I'll be sure to ask the funeral director today if she has any.'

Baby James, who was sitting beside Mum on the bed, let out a giggle too, that infectious 'no idea what I'm laughing at, but you're laughing too so I will laugh' laugh.

Mum gave him a little poke in the ribs. 'What are you laughing at, James Tosca?' which only made him laugh more, until he fell back on the pillow. I stopped laughing. In a split second the emotional pendulum had swung back, to remind me that James would never remember his nana or her laugh.

She wore Red Hot Red

Mum was a big fan of the prepaid funeral, decisions made by the very person whom it concerns. She'd made a call to the funeral director earlier in the year but nothing had actually been put in place; the time had come. I suspect that it's easier to plan a funeral when it's expected to be a few years away. Discussing a plan that was likely to be put in place in a few days was certain to be more emotional but Mum knew it was better than leaving us to make decisions in the shadow of grief, especially if it could be avoided.

Deb greeted Mum with warmth when she came to her bedside.

'Hello, Pamela,' she said, grabbing her hand. The two had liaised many times over the years when Mum's business provided flowers to adorn caskets. Mum was already propped up on the fluffy pillows ready to make the decisions needed, quickly and without fuss. She had perfect clarity and was in complete control. Deb retrieved a thick folder from her briefcase.

'Pamela, I know you want to organise as much as possible so I will need you to select a casket.' She opened the folder that revealed pictures of the many different kinds available.

'I don't want to spend unnecessary money on a coffin, recycled cardboard is fine, it's going up in flames anyway.'

Deb laughed. 'OK.'

Despite the decision being made we spent a few minutes flicking through the pages gasping at some of the ornate coffins available, including one that was gold plated and cost around $50,000.

'Who in God's name pays that much for a coffin?' asked Mum.

'Gangsters do.' I laughed. 'One who got murdered a few months ago was in one of those, but I didn't know it cost that much.'

We flicked to the picture of the cheapest coffin on offer, the recycled cardboard.

'It's certainly understated,' remarked Mum.

My response wasn't as reserved. 'It's ugly! What will people think? I'm not getting you a gold coffin but are you sure we shouldn't splash out a little, move up a level? We're going to look like tight-arses,' I teased.

'No,' she insisted. 'What a waste.'

'Are you sure it will even be able to hold you without disintegrating? What if it gets wet?' I mocked.

Deb was clearly amused. 'There is nothing to worry about, they're actually very robust. Did you want to decorate it?'

'Yes we'd like to but we can't decide on the best way to do it. Mum would like the children to do it on the day but I'm worried that in the real world this would end in lots of scribbles and prove distracting during the service.'

'That's OK. I'll just get the casket delivered to you beforehand so that you can all decorate it in a controlled environment. I could get it here anytime you wish, as early as tomorrow.'

Problem solved. I smiled, turning to Mum. 'Well there you go, your dream will become a reality, your grandchildren will get to make your box beautiful.'

The questions that followed were fairly straightforward. Where would the funeral service be held? Had we made contact with the priest? And when asked if we would like to arrange a viewing, Mum's directive was firm: 'Once I'm gone, I'm gone, that's it. There will be absolutely no viewing by anyone.'

Deb took note whilst moving on through her list. 'No doubt there will be flowers, I assume you'll want to take care of that.'

Mum's answer sounded a little odd, considering she was a florist. 'No, I don't want any flowers in the church. I would like a circle of gardenias on my coffin, like Princess Di. Classic and simple.'

Two occasions that demand lots of flowers are weddings and funerals, but not for my mother. A florist who carried a prayer book and rosary beads on her wedding day instead of a wedding bouquet, and at her funeral there would nothing but a single wreath.

Before Deb could suggest that people be asked to donate to a charity in lieu of flowers, Mum added, 'Oh, and I don't want to ask people to donate money instead of sending flowers. I don't like asking people to do that, they will donate what they can when they can, they don't need me asking them to do it.'

'What about music? We have several musicians we can put you in touch with,' and Deb handed over another folder.

I looked down the list and read it to Mum. 'There's a cellist, a violin quartet, a harpist.'

'A harp would be nice,' Mum said, and another decision was made. 'Deb, I'd also like my niece's daughter to sing if she is happy to.'

The question of what she was going to sing, though, remained unanswered. I made a note on my list of things to do: *Hymns? Songs? Final song???*

Nothing we had discussed seemed morbid. On the contrary, it had felt constructive and proactive, but that all changed with the next question.

'Have you chosen pallbearers?'

Despite the care with which the question was delivered, the ever-so-slight pause in Mum's response was overwhelming. I forced myself to look down so as to not meet anyone's eyes.

Every funeral I had been to was slightly different, but regardless of whether the death was of a woman, man or child, whether they were elderly or young, a coffin being carried by loved ones was always the part where even the most stoic would 'crack'. There is something so regal and emotional about the final act.

I remember when new OH&S laws within the industry had meant pallbearers from funeral homes changed to wheeling the coffin out on a trolley. It's not the same and it was never ever a consideration for us. What good would three striking big sons be if not to carry our mother on her final journey?

'My sons and my son-in-law will be the pallbearers.' There was a poignant silence. All of a sudden the death of my mother felt real, and my chest tightened. I didn't know what to say or where to look but thankfully Mum took control and continued. 'And I want my family to say goodbye to me at the church. Strictly no one is to go to the crematorium. I don't want anyone distraught as my coffin goes behind the curtain, that would be terrible.'

The air was thick with emotion. There was no room for humour and I kept quiet. How Deb and her peers had such conversations day in day out was beyond me but she was the consummate professional. With just the right amount of everything she moved the meeting forward.

'Do you know what you'd like to be dressed in?' It was a topic that helped shift the mood. Mum's face broke into a wry smile as I shared the unlikely and unfortunate story of the white nightie. It turned out that Mum had been wearing the gown when the catheter was being inserted and in an effort to make it easier Jayne had grabbed a pair of scissors and, using an old nursing trick, cut it up the back. A whole wardrobe full of clothes and the one item Mum requested to be cremated in had been butchered. 'Typical,' Mum had said when I told her the fate of her chosen coffin wear. Jayne, however, was mortified and promised to sew it back up.

'Well, I think that's it! Everything else I can work out with Kellie and the family later. Is there any other request I can help you with, Pamela?' Deb's words were kind but her eyes even more so.

'Yes,' Mum said. 'Can I have a bottle of scotch placed in the coffin, please?' Another perfectly delivered circuit breaker! All three of us welcomed the laugh.

'Mmm, I don't know how the bottle would fare once it hits the fire,' said Deb through her chuckle.

'OK, maybe not,' was Mum's dry reply. As the giggle petered out I noticed that Deb's eyes had welled. It made me want to cry for her. I guess even when discussing coffins is part of your day job, you never become immune.

The local priest was mid prayer at Mum's bedside when I arrived back from running errands. I put down my things and joined in, though it did feel a little odd. It had been years since a priest had made a visit to our family at home; our days as practising Catholics had fallen by the wayside two decades ago. Mum was brought up a fairly strict Catholic, attending mass several times a week, and as a young family we never missed Sunday mass. Mum dressed us in our best outfits, which were colour coordinated with hers; my favourite was a black sleeveless dress with tiny white dots and white lace trim with a small brooch at the neck, long white socks, black patent Mary Jane shoes and a white wide-brimmed hat. The boys were in opposite coloured shorts and trousers. At nine am on the seventh day of every week with very few exceptions we would take up our unofficial position in the second pew of our local church. It was the only time I ever heard Mum's lovely singing. Despite looking like angels we would moan about having to go and we were bribed with the promise of a chocolate milkshake if we behaved. Dad would meet us at the milkbar for the reward, as most Sunday mornings he was conveniently held up at the stables with track work.

For years Mum was head of the parish group and each week created floral arrangements for the church altar. My brothers were altar boys and I was one of the very first altar girls in the area, but once we hit our early teens and had a say in whether we went to mass, it all seemed to die off. For Mum, Flowers by Pamela, the shop she had opened when I was fifteen, required her to work six days a week, and the church ritual became spasmodic at best. In later years even the sacred days of Christmas and Easter Sunday went 'to God', so to speak.

When the priest finished his blessing and had given Mum communion I introduced myself. He then asked whether we had given thought to the funeral service. 'Would you like a full mass, Pamela?'

I was about to answer for Mum and tell the priest that we wanted to keep it simple with the shorter version when Mum spoke. 'Yes, I would like a full mass.'

Really? I thought. 'Are you sure, Mum, you want the whole shebang?'

'Yes.'

'OK,' I said in a bemused tone. 'It's your funeral.' No one laughed.

The priest began to make us aware of the obligations that came with wanting a full mass, such as certain readings from the scriptures and appropriate hymns. I started to feel a little uneasy at the direction in which the conversation was headed as the man was clearly going by the book. I'd assumed because he was once a reverend of a different faith that he would be progressive. I'd assumed wrong.

'Father, Mum likes a song from the seventies that we thought could be a bit of fun. It's called "Some Girls Will".'

The priest didn't crack a smile, and whether he knew the song we were referring to or not the answer was a firm, 'No, that's not appropriate.' I made a mental note to tackle that one later but it was time for more pressing decisions.

'I believe you wish to be cremated, Pamela.'

I had always known Mum wanted to be cremated. The thought of her children crying over a headstone in the ground was something she found abhorrent. It was what she had done for years at her own mother's grave. Whilst the raw pain and physical tears subsided, the feeling of obligation to visit the cemetery never faded. At least my father's parents were by sheer coincidence just a few plots away and until we were in our teens, every Christmas, Easter, and Mother's Day we would take flowers to lay for 'Little Nana', 'Big Nana' and a few others. No one visits anymore, no one.

'We have a lovely memorial wall in a garden within our church grounds,' suggested the priest.

'That sounds fine,' said Mum. I wasn't sure if she actually meant it or whether she was being polite, because she had often said she'd like to be scattered on the ocean. What's the difference between a memorial wall and a gravesite? I'd still feel like I had to visit it. I couldn't hold my tongue.

'Yes that sounds lovely, Father, but only some of the ashes will go in there. I would like some to go on the garden Mum created for me at my home, and so would one of my brothers.'

With little expression and no indication of a compromise the man of the cloth responded, 'We believe it is sacrilegious to separate the body parts. They should remain intact.'

I said nothing but a loud rant was taking place inside my head. We're not dismembering her, you fool, they're ashes, she will be gone. Why are we bothering to even tell you? How would you know whether the box contained all her ashes? How would you even know if they were hers at all?

Mum's eyes locked with mine. Her ever-so-slightly raised eyebrows suggested she might have been thinking the same but her silence indicated that she was not going to argue. Her look said, 'Let it go.'

That's it! I decided then and there that the priest and his rigid ways weren't for us. In my mind we would finish the meeting, thank him for his time and blessing and find someone else. I was sure Mum would agree to ditching him.

The arrival of my brother Steve was the perfect interruption. An imposing but friendly six-foot-two figure, he walked in and immediately extended his hand to the priest. 'Hello, Father, I'm Steve and I should tell you I'm eternal.'

I started to chuckle and Mum couldn't help but smile. The blank look on the priest's face showed he was not even holding the same book as us, let alone in with a chance of being on the same page. He left, offering to return whenever Mum would like.

'Well, that went well!' I said sarcastically as soon as he was gone, and I floated the idea of changing churches and priest. I was fired up. 'This is not what you want, Mum. I want you to have the service you want. If it includes Racey's "Some Girls Will" being played then it should be.'

But she was tired and like on so many occasions during those days she uttered three words: 'It doesn't matter.'

'OK.' I nodded but there was no way I was letting it go. Where there was a will there must be a way, though at that point I had no real idea what it was.

She wore Fuchsia Shock

McKenzie pondered the range of different flowers for sale before pointing to a bright bunch of multi-coloured tulips.

'I want to give Nana these!' she said.

'They're lovely but I thought you wanted roses.'

'No. I like the tulips.'

She also had a change of heart when it came to choosing the fairy she wanted to buy Nana to take to heaven. The clearance store was a treasure trove of odds and ends with a small selection of garden trinkets, but the winged creatures were passed over for a happy-looking ornamental ant that sat upright on a ceramic pink flower with a yellow centre. McKenzie cupped it with both hands and carried it over to the card section.

I watched her look long and hard at the small selection of goodbye cards. One had rainbows, some had love hearts. I waited for her to make a choice. I was barely able to hold it together when I saw her small hand reach up and pull out a thank-you card. 'This one,' she said, with a satisfied smile.

We went to a café for hot chocolate and as we sat down at a table for two I felt the 'mother guilt' of never spending one-on-one time with my children. No wonder they loved their treat day with Nana. I smiled at my seven-year-old, who seemed so big and who'd all but put her whole face into the warm chocolate liquid, and just when I thought she was at risk of drowning in it she looked up. 'Will anyone else be at Nana's when we go?' I wasn't sure whether she meant visitors or family but she continued before I could answer. 'I don't want anyone else there, I want to be alone with Nana.' She then opened the pack of pencils we had bought and began to write on the card. The only guidance she sought was the spelling of a few words.

When she had finished she showed it to me. Aware I was being watched I held back the tears that were busting to be released. 'That's beautiful, darling,' I said, and we set off for our date with Nana, who was waiting.

Mum was sitting up against the pillows with a bag of lollies by the bed and Mary-Ann had helped her put bright lipstick on.

'Hi, Nana,' said McKenzie, with an almost alarming degree of normality. She handed over her offerings and Mum admired the bright blooms and the ant.

'How did you know I needed an ant?'

McKenzie shrugged with satisfaction. 'I'll put them here on the table near the window so you can look at them.'

If my girl was shocked by the physical deterioration of her beloved Nana she gave nothing away. I watched her cuddle in the arms that had held her since the hour she was born. She rubbed her hand softly back and forth over the soft silver stubble that had grown back on Mum's head. 'Nana, I think your hair is starting to grow again.'

'Do you think?' Mum said, engaging her eldest grandchild in light banter about her day.

A few minutes later McKenzie redirected the questions back to Mum. 'Why are your eyes yellow, Nana?'

I quietly left the room whilst two very good friends talked effortlessly as they usually did. A few minutes later I popped my head in to check all was OK, and McKenzie asked me to read her card out loud to Nana, the words of a little girl's wise head but heavy heart. 'Dear Nana, I am going to miss you when you die and I will see you today. Thank you for being the best Nana in the world. From McKenzie with love.'

It was then that McKenzie lay across her grandmother's chest and began to sob, 'I don't want you to die.'

There was nothing that could have stopped my tears or the sound of my child's heart shattering into pieces. I didn't know what to say and I had no idea what Mum was going to come up with but I was sure as hell hoping she was going to say something. Mum's heartache was visible; this was clearly the most significant and painful stage of the entire journey. She tightened her grip around McKenzie, whose head was still buried in her chest, and waited a few moments before tenderly telling her the simple but honest truth: 'I don't want to die either, my darling. I don't want to leave you. But my body is sick and it can't get better and I need to go to heaven.'

The sobs continued for a little longer and then stopped abruptly. I thought McKenzie was going to ask another question to help her understand or give her reassurance but instead she stood up and calmly said, 'I want to go home now.' She kissed her nana goodbye and I took her into the kitchen.

With no clue what to say I made a desperate and futile attempt to make a bad situation better by offering her something she was usually denied. 'Would you like a Coke?'

Her sobs instantly returned with force. 'I don't want a Coke! I don't want anything.'

I wrapped my arms around her as we left to go home; when we got outside I asked her, 'What can I do to make you feel better?'

It was then she let out what could only be described as a primal cry. 'Nothing is going to make me feel better ever again.'

She was right! Nothing was going to fix that moment, so we stood on the footpath and cried.

The advice that had come back from the very people who deal with children and grief regularly was that there were no rules. I knew it was OK for the children to see me cry as it would allow them to feel free to express their emotions, and a child psychologist reinforced this. But I was also convinced that it was crucial the children visit Nana to say goodbye; not literally, but to see her for a final time to say 'I love you'. The most valuable guidance I received was to listen to what my children were saying and to be careful not to ignore their wishes. If they didn't want to visit Nana, I shouldn't force the issue. It was suggested I try to explain the circle of living and dying, using phrases like, 'Sometimes people get sick and can't get better.' I hadn't relayed this to Mum and yet she had said almost those exact words to McKenzie when she became upset at the thought of Mum dying. And how bizarre that my child had asked to buy an ornament Nana could take to heaven, not knowing that the professionals had suggested exactly that.

In a spontaneous flashback I vividly remembered having a similar sentiment when my father had died two days after his fifty-seventh birthday. I had bought him a card several months before but had forgotten about it and never gave it to him. For some reason I remembered it the day after he died. It had a line of old-fashioned English soldiers poised with guns in the air and a 'happy birthday' greeting. On the inside the guns were revealed to be popguns and the words said: 'Don't pop off too soon.' When we went to view his body I slipped the card inside the suit he was dressed in.

So it would seem that McKenzie's beautiful but distressing visit with Nana was very normal. Why was it that I felt like it had gone completely awry? And was that how we were supposed to leave it? What about Sidney and Stella? They were also now asking to be taken shopping for flowers and fairies to visit Nana, but did I really want a repeat of what my eldest child had just experienced? I was desperate to get it right until I came to the realisation that there wasn't a 'right' to get.

She wore Passionata Pink

The 'good periods' had deteriorated into ten-minute blocks and were progressively happening later in the day as her body clock became confused. There were some benefits to the late-night wakefulness. It was quiet and we got to talk, a glimpse of blissful normality that I had taken for granted my whole life. How the hell did we get to this?

Mary-Ann said Mum had no memory of McKenzie's time with her earlier that afternoon, but when the brief 'wake' period came I hinted at what had occurred and she whispered, 'I know,' with perfect recollection of every heartbreaking sob. It was hard knowing she knew exactly what was going on but it was also reassurance that I still had time for us to talk; above all else I just needed to be able to talk to her.

When a window of opportunity opened later that night I sat down with her and with my notebook and a video recorder. Mum was less than thrilled that there would be footage of her looking her absolute worst, but I told her that it wasn't for her, it was for the children and me. Whilst I was seemingly operating like someone who had it all together, one day in the coming months or years when I got a chance to process it all I would have forgotten things and I didn't want to forget.

I opened the notebook to my 'to know' list. I already knew the big milestones but there were lots of little things I didn't. I never knew the origins of each string of pearls that I was about to be entrusted with. Some had been my grandmother's; pieces of my great-grandfather's fob-watch chain were crafted into another set.

'Where did the topaz ring come from?' I asked.

'I bought that with my first pay cheque, my first significant purchase.' It was a big rectangle in a high setting that I had never really liked but on learning its origin I instantly developed a soft spot for it. We laughed about the fur coats in the closet that she used to wear proudly to Sunday mass. How times had changed: few would be game to wear those now. One of my favourites in the collection wasn't church wear but it was the most glamorous. The white fox stole had belonged to the mother of her best friend Susie, who had given it to Mum because she knew she would use it, and for many years she did. As a little girl I would wrap it around my shoulders and dance around the room striking ballerina poses.

'What's your favourite childhood memory?' I asked.

'Ballet lessons as a child.' She smiled as if catching a glimpse. Mum's love of ballet was one of the reasons she had encouraged my classical ballet lessons that began when I was five. I'd really wanted to do tap dancing but she'd insisted tap wasn't classy enough. I knew she'd been a talented dancer, though wasn't aware that as a teenager she'd been offered a scholarship to the Australian Ballet Guild. 'I dropped out because I didn't feel like I was good enough.'

I yearned for more detail about snippets of things I remembered but needed her to fill in the blanks. How did she meet Dad? Where had he proposed? I'd imagined a romantic setting. 'I was on the outside loo when he came outside to find me, then when I came out he proposed,' she said with a faint smile.

Mum had a brief stint on television in her early twenties but I didn't know that it had been on a morning show doing exercises of all things. I had memories of a black-and-white image of Mum with Rat Pack legend

Sammy Davis Junior, which had been dragged out a few times over the years, and knew that he had said to her, 'You call me Sammy and I'll call you Pammie,' but I was surprised to learn that she'd chauffeured the car he was in as part of her public relations role for a rental car company.

My questions flip-flopped between nostalgic and practical but no matter how random they were, answers were forthcoming. I made a note of when she developed asthma and the endless list of allergies that included eggs, fish, and animal hair. It would all be useful information if anyone in the family developed sensitivities at a later date.

'If you had your time again, what would you do differently?' I could see her ponder before answering. 'I wouldn't change anything that happened.' I sensed there was a 'but' coming, though I had no idea what it would be. 'But I'm sorry I didn't tell you all more often how wonderful and beautiful you all were.' I'd heard that lament a handful of times in recent years. Mum had encouraged us as kids and gave generous credit when it was due but her nurturing also included honest appraisal. On the other hand she recalled friends who'd told their kids how fabulous or beautiful they were even when perhaps conventionally they weren't.

'I thought I was doing the right thing by not letting you get big-headed or develop an unrealistic opinion of yourselves, but I was wrong. Those children who were constantly being told how brilliant and fabulous they were, it didn't matter if it was true, they believed it to be true and developed an unshakeable belief in themselves.'

'You will be beautiful one day,' is what my mother would say to me as an insecure and unsure adolescent. Pictures will show I was a pretty little girl until the age of nine but I can almost pinpoint the day when things went pear-shaped, or rather when I did. Teenage hormones were typically unkind without being too cruel, and I remember that my mother wrapped her arms around me in a bearhug, kissed my head and whispered, 'Your time will come.' But I wanted to know when. As if there was a predetermined date when I would blossom. It seemed that she was right about most things so I trusted she would be on that too. 'You're only beautiful once,' she cautioned, in an effort to offer comfort that I hadn't used my turn of being pretty too early. My awkward teenage self was in awe of my mother's confidence. Whatever insecurities she may have harboured about her scarred hands or other imperfections, I hoped I would one day be as beautiful as her. 'You have good foundations, we can easily fix or fudge the rest,' she assured me, but I couldn't help envy 'natural' beauties.

There was a girl a few years older than me who lived down the road from us; she was tall with beautiful eyes and very blonde almost white hair, flawless skin, a Marilyn Monroe beauty spot and a chipped front tooth that added rather than detracted from her charm. 'She is a true natural beauty that one,' my mother remarked to me after passing her one day.

'Will I be that beautiful one day?' I asked, though it was a loaded question. Without a hint of sarcasm or malice came her reply: 'I don't think so.' My reaction was one of hurt and outrage but Mum didn't try to backpedal. 'No matter how beautiful you are, no matter how smart or rich you are, there will always be someone more beautiful, smarter and richer and there will always be someone with less than you. That's life.'

I'm sure she immediately regretted having served her truthful thoughts 'raw' rather than warm but her explanation was a life lesson she figured I would learn sooner or later, along with one of her other favourite clichés: 'Beauty is in the eye of the beholder.'

It made me sad to think she felt that she had in some way failed us. 'We turned out OK, Mum.'

'I know,' she said, 'I could not be more proud.'

I felt a large lump in my throat.

'Do you have any regrets?'

There was a reflective pause. 'Not learning to say no earlier.'

'What's your favourite memory?'

Mum's answer was instant: 'All of you as babies,' she beamed. She'd always said we were her greatest achievement, even though collectively we had achieved finding careers among the least trusted professions. There had never been any pressure on us to be anything in particular; maybe a little more pressure during our school years might have done us all good, and led to more successful academic outcomes. Even when the dismal school reports would come home there was never anger or disappointment at our lack of scholastic attainment; neither she nor Dad finished secondary school. Raising one eyebrow, Mum read out loud a comment from a report received midway through my high-school years: 'A delightful student who shows very little interest in her work.' The same set of neat eyebrows were raised again as she heard me making a futile attempt to bluff Dad into thinking the 'G' I had received for science the same year was for 'good'.

Dad would rant and rave about the waste of bloody expensive school fees but not Mum. 'I don't care what you end up doing in life as long as you're happy.' I couldn't count how many times I heard Mum say it. We may have lacked academically but just like our parents we more than made the grade with our work ethic and street smarts and all had part-time jobs from a young age. At thirteen I was working at the local ice-cream parlour and was thrilled to be paid the princely sum of $3.25 an hour. With my first pay, I bought Mum a bunch of pink carnations from a roadside stall. She had kept just about every trinket that any of us had bought for her with our hard-earned cash, no matter how garish they were. Even Dad had liked buying Mum useless gadgets and humorous gifts.

I laughed as I began to recall a few of our favourites. 'Remember the chocolate that was in the shape of a record? On the outside it said "Just for the record I love you".'

'What about the wooden back scratcher?' A smile tickled Mum's face just before the small window of talk time closed again.

I turned the pages of the A4 spiral workbook I was writing in and realised it was becoming an unintended and disjointed family chronicle; despite its aesthetics it would be an invaluable keepsake. A few pages from the back was my 'to do' list. I scanned down the ticks and lines through the items that had needed to be actioned: coffin, music, lawyer and priest, the list was complete. Everything – well, all the really important things that needed doing – was now done; we were now 'waiting'.

It was my turn to stay the night with Mum. I planned to sleep in her bed right next to her, though I knew there would be no sleep. I wanted to hear and feel every breath in case one of them happened to be her last.

Goodness knows what made me think the end was near, but I had a sixth sense that the loose ends were tied, that all the important issues had been addressed and she would choose that night to slip away. Black Friday, I reminded myself; it would somehow be fitting that it should be the end.

Sometime after midnight the house was quiet but I could sense she was awake. It was just like the movies and in spite of myself I delivered a near perfect cliché. 'It's OK to go, Mum, everything is in order now, it's OK to go.'

A few seconds passed and I wondered if I'd been wrong, perhaps she was asleep, then she spoke. 'Go where?'

'Oh, you're not funny,' I growled. In a selfless moment of telling her it was OK to die, she decided it was an apt time to make a joke. 'I'm telling you that it's OK to die, for goodness sake. I'm telling you it's all right, that you don't have to hang on for us anymore.'

To which she replied in a very matter-of-fact but convincing tone: 'I'm going to die on Tuesday.'

'Oh, well, why didn't you say?' I sarcastically retorted. 'What's so special about Tuesday?'

As if it was glaringly obvious she pointed out that her GP and Dr John would be back from holidays on that day. I couldn't really see the relevance, given that neither of them was officially in charge of her care, but I let it slide.

As the night ticked by very slowly I found that it was her stroking my head, asking if I was OK. The darkness made it all feel so much heavier and I broke under its virtual weight. There was no withholding my childlike heaving sobs, and Mum's sadness, though not visible, was palpable. We both knew that despite her dignified and realistic approach to death there would be no escaping the void that she would leave. I confessed that above all things I was fearful of how desperately lonely I would be without having her to talk to. She was my sounding board for everything, even if I hadn't liked what she had to say.

'We've done the hard yards,' she said.

The hard yards? 'What do you mean the hard yards?' I piped up, almost taking offence 'Which part of it was so hard?'

She paused and then said, 'None of it! None of it was too hard.' There was another brief silence. 'You are my life.'

Why is it after a good cry you can have such a deep sleep? And I did. Mum had declared that she wouldn't be dying that night and there was not one single reason to believe she'd be wrong. I shut my eyes, knowing my mother as she had my whole life was watching over me.

Black Friday superstition didn't manifest a poetic death and I woke feeling relieved but also with a sense of being in limbo. Everyone was watching for the signs that would signal the imminent end, but when the end takes longer than you think the mental goodbyes end up becoming like Groundhog Day. We couldn't plan for a recovery so there was little choice but to enter into a holding pattern, and we sat in the kitchen in shifts, drinking tea or wine.

My aunt or brothers were on watch whilst I made good on my promise to Sidney and took her for hot chocolate and to choose flowers and a card for Nana. We stumbled across some decorative stones, perfect for the fairy garden. As if by fate there were four different designs. One had a blue dragonfly with the word 'Dream', another was a ladybug and its word was 'Happiness', there was a bee inscribed with 'Hope' and the last was an orange dragonfly with 'Love'. We bought two of each. The four children would be able to give Nana one each then hang onto its twin as a keepsake.

Sidney couldn't wait to have her 'alone' time with Nana and show her the bright mixed posy of flowers she had chosen. It was only a day since McKenzie's visit but Mum's decline was significant. The brightest lipstick wasn't enough to disguise what was happening, though it didn't stop Mum trying. 'Hello, my darling B.'

Our family had called Sidney 'B' almost since she was born. McKenzie had been unable to pronounce her new sister's name so she called her 'Baby'; not long after it was shortened to 'B' and it stuck.

I could see that Sidney was overwhelmed at the sight of her sick Nana, though she tried desperately to put on a brave face. She gave Nana a hug and handed over her flowers and the pebble that had the bumblebee. 'Oh it's a bee from B,' said Mum.

Sidney beamed. 'And Mum bought me a hot chocolate!' she said. They began to talk about school and ballet and other daily happenings but as I went to leave the room Sidney grabbed my hand and whispered, 'I'm scared! Don't go.' Her reaction was understandable but it still hurt all the same, and we only stayed a few minutes more. 'Bye, Nan,' she said, planting a kiss on Mum's forehead as if she would be back tomorrow for afternoon tea.

'Goodbye darling,' Mum replied, and my little girl and I walked home.

Stella's visit later that day brought unexpected relief, not because I thought she was better at coping with seeing Mum's condition, but because I believed she was incapable of really understanding what was happening. To my three-year-old very little would get in the way of a bag of lollies, and despite all that was going on Nana still had her bright lipstick freshly applied and a bag of sweets by her bed. Stella handed over the red roses she had chosen, happily parted with the precious stone that was in her perfect chubby hand and became blissfully focused on how much sugar she could get into her mouth before I told her, 'That's enough.'

I was so focused on being ready to console and hold either or both of my two younger daughters in the event their visits went down a similar path to their big sister's that I never considered how painful it must have been for Mum. Perhaps she was also concentrating more on their wellbeing like she always did.

I was tired and somewhat relieved when the visits were done, but as soon as Stella and I arrived home

McKenzie asked if she could see Nana again to hand over her special stone. Given her near collapse last time we visited and knowing Mum had further deteriorated I did have reservations but then agreed anyway. I put my jacket back on and walked her back down the path to Nana's house.

Who would have thought that my eldest girl would display an almost ethereal calm. She wasn't overwhelmed by Nana's decline, she was warm, loving and talkative. With great pride she presented her little grey garden pebble, the little red ladybug with 'Happiness' written on it. There was no space left on the small table with three vases of flowers, three cards, one garden ant and four bright garden stones ready and waiting to go on Nana's journey to heaven.

'I'd like a photo with Nana,' McKenzie said out of the blue. I didn't ask why and McKenzie didn't give a reason, though I looked at Mum with raised eyebrows and she responded with a dry, 'Oh, great.' McKenzie lay on the bed and nestled her head right next to her nana; she couldn't get any closer and the moment was captured. There wasn't a hint of sadness or the desperation she'd displayed last time. Instead she planted a light kiss on Nana's cheek. 'Bye, Nana Pana.'

Nana Pana was a nickname the grandchildren had often called Mum. It had started one day when they were trying to think of rhyming words. It was light-hearted fun and I hadn't heard anyone say it for weeks. At the doorway to the bedroom McKenzie looked back and gave her nana a wave and a smile.

Looking back at the pictures on the camera, there was a photo as beautiful as you could ever see. My little girl was looking adoringly at her nana, a grin from ear to ear. This was love.

She wore Silverspun Rose

'You know I'm going to go to a psychic after you're gone, don't you.'

There was no element of surprise in Mum's reply. 'I know.'

Mum and I had loved seeing the odd psychic, or medium. We weren't obsessed by them nor did we take their readings as gospel, but we did enjoy the whole concept. There were none that had really blown us away, though, until we met Audrey.

She was the least likely 'spook' I'd ever seen – more like a lovely grandma from a storybook, soft and pretty. When I walked into her front room it was drenched in sunlight, and hundreds if not thousands of blown-glass figurines were scattered around the room. We sat opposite each other but with not much space between us and in a quiet voice she began.

'You've just come back from overseas … You've had something to do with advertising, I think … You're going to run into someone you haven't seen for a while.'

I was twenty-three years old at the time and whilst I had been overseas and worked in advertising the sceptic in me wasn't overly impressed. She told me I had a friend who had just broken up from a long-term relationship and I was to give her the message that 'apples will grow again'.

At the end of our time allocation I got up to leave when Audrey stopped me. 'Just a moment, dear. Is your father alive?'

'No,' I replied.

'Is he a tall man who wears a long coat and a peaked cap?'

Well that's what Dad used to wear to morning track work, so I answered, 'Yes.'

'He has just entered the room and is standing behind your right shoulder.'

I felt a shudder. Not because I felt my father over my shoulder but because I was scared of what was going to come out of her mouth next.

'Sit back down.' For the next few minutes she told me about my father, that he was happy, that he missed his family. I remained seated but unmoved. The clincher came when she started to 'hum'. I thought that the sweet old lady had 'lost it', as she pressed on.

'I can't quite make out the tune,' she said, clearly frustrated. 'La la la.' She was actually trying to hum a tune. 'Oh, that's it!' she said with satisfaction. 'He is singing "Little Brown Jug".'

I started to cry. How would anyone know that the first song I taught myself to play on the organ we had at home when I was around ten was in fact the Glenn Miller tune 'Little Brown Jug'? At that moment, if Audrey had told me to write a cheque for my small life's savings I would have done it. I was 'sold'. As far as I was concerned my dad was in the building.

I couldn't wait to get home and tell Mum, and drove straight to her shop. Of course Mum immediately made an appointment and went to see Audrey a week later, and whilst she didn't get any 'humming' or people entering the room, she was still fairly impressed by the woman with the 'glass menagerie'.

So given our measured intrigue of those with 'connections to the other side' there was nothing surer than that I would be going in search of Mum when she had gone.

'You don't need a psychic to know that I am with you. Look at those babies; that's where I am going to be.'

'I know. That's profound and all that but frankly not enough. I wonder how long I should wait before I go in search of someone to find you? In any case, what we need is a code.'

I decided we would need a word. 'It has to be a word that only you and I know. I will not tell a living soul. That way I will be sure it's you coming through.'

'OK,' she said as she rolled her eyes. 'You choose the word.'

There was no science in selecting the code word, no emotion or sentimental link, it was just a word. I also proposed a back-up phrase just in case she couldn't remember the word. We laughed.

A soft silence followed, which led me to think that our window of talk time had closed, but I was wrong.

'You know, I didn't give you a birthday card this year. The first time in your life I haven't bought you a card. I'm sorry.'

'As if I care. Don't worry about it!' I said, without realising that the birthday card I'd never received would have been the last one I would have ever received from her. It wouldn't have been much different from her cards from every other year: 'To my darling daughter' would be written at the top, and underneath the printed 'Happy Birthday' would be 'Your loving mother', but suddenly I felt her sadness. Was it really just five weeks earlier we had celebrated our birthdays at Taco Bill's? Why hadn't we given more thought to the fact that it was certainly her last birthday? Twelve months earlier there had been a catered lunch and a surprise party. What a difference a year made. My own birthday would never be the same; the day before would always be her birthday and it would forever mark her absence.

Whilst I was busy ticking off my list of important things to know, Mum was clearly mentally ticking off her list as well. 'Don't forget to go and get the jewellery cleaned,' she said out of the blue.

'Good on you, Mum,' I scoffed. 'I'm sitting here planning ways to contact you in the afterlife and you're thinking about getting your jewellery cleaned.'

'I meant to take it weeks ago, can you take it tomorrow?' she asked as if she was doing nothing more than a little housekeeping.

I gave in. 'OK. Where is it?'

'It's under the couch.'

'You hid it under the couch? Great! When were you going to tell me that?' I would have stressed that someone may have stolen it.

'I'm telling you now,' she said as I got down on my knees to sweep my hand under the couch, finding the small boxes containing all her trinkets, the pearls, several dress rings and earrings, some valuable some not.

When I was little I loved playing dress-ups with her clothes, make-up, high heels and jewellery. Somehow I ended up looking like a bejewelled drag queen but it provided me with endless hours of pleasure.

Her charm bracelet was a tangible timeline. Dad had bought her all but a few of the forty or so pieces that dangled from the gold chain. As I turned it through my fingers it sounded like a soft wind chime and nostalgia swept over me with memories of the pieces that had mesmerised us as kids. The little telephone with the dial made out of tiny garnets that actually moved round, a tiny teapot that had an even smaller lid, which lifted on and off, and the British soldier that could move in and out of his guardhouse. I had also bought a few in places I had travelled in my late teens, that's how long it had been since a new charm was added.

I picked up the diamond earrings Mum had bought herself. She'd had her ears pierced when she turned fifty, and soon after spoilt her lobes with 'bling'. It reminded me of how I had pleaded with her from the age of ten to allow me to have my ears pierced. The answer was fixed at 'No'. By the time I was old enough to make my own decision I no longer wanted it done and was amused that she did.

'Why don't you go to the pharmacy and get your ears done?' Mum said as I placed the earrings back in their box.

I laughed at the change in her tune that had come thirty years too late. Funnily enough I had no interest, even if I was guaranteed to receive bling. 'Nope.'

Humorous irony was replaced by a swell of sadness that rose through my chest. I had always known the jewellery would be mine one day but I suddenly realised the handover was taking place. But the pieces weren't mine; they never would be. I would forever see them as my mother's even when I eventually handed them on to my own daughters. That would be a whole other unenviable task to look forward to. When there is only one daughter there are no decisions to be made. When you have three daughters the divvy-up would be a dangerous game. I felt my stomach turn, but it wasn't for that day in the future, it was another realisation. Something was missing.

'Mum, where is the aquamarine ring and pendant?'

She was dozing on and off but managed a very calm, 'They're there.'

Trying not to show any alarm I insisted, 'No, they're not!'

It occurred to me that because her short-term memory was somewhat affected perhaps she wasn't able to remember. My bigger concern was that if she died before I found them or before she remembered they might have been lost for a long time.

'Did you lend them to anyone, Mum?'

'No, they're under the couch.'

I got on my knees again and looked underneath the couch. Nothing was there. The window of opportunity closed again and she slept. I put the boxes back under the couch.

She wore Paint the Town Pink

It was a Sunday morning reminiscent of our youth, when one of my brothers rode his bike to fetch the papers. It was a standard order: the *Sunday Observer*, the *Sunday Press* and the *Sunday Telegraph*. The leftover change was payment to the paperboy, who spent it on lollies or a sneaky packet of cigarettes to smoke at the park with naughty friends. When the papers made it home our family would scatter over the couches and carpet to look at them. This secured a good thirty minutes of 'quiet' in an otherwise very loud house.

That morning in our mother's house the traditional roles were assumed and Robert went off to collect the papers and the bread rolls. It was a different backdrop but the scene was very familiar: the papers strewn across the floor in various sections were dispersed depending on interests and then rotated. The crossword belonged to Mum. That day it remained untouched.

The hours passed slowly as Mum's wakeful periods continued to diminish. Whatever she managed though was still coherent and purposeful. The afternoon was also a lot like the Sunday afternoons of our childhood. There was nothing that urgently needing doing, nowhere anyone had to be but exactly where we were.

I was in the countdown of our final conversations and we both knew it, but 'I love you' had been said a million times so our exchange returned to everyday 'natter'. It was actually me doing the nattering about the kids, her adding a word here and there and smiling. It almost seemed a waste of valuable time, but what else would we have done?

I continued to ask for more specifics regarding her funeral. We had covered the big issues but addressing as many of the finer details as we could meant there was less I would have to ponder later. We talked about her death like we were discussing one day in the future, except that the future was going to be a reality very soon, and if it was on her schedule it would be in two days.

'I thought maybe you'd like to have "Perhaps Love" played at the service.'

'Yes, that's lovely.'

The song, sung by John Denver and Placido Domingo, was such a pretty tune. I'd used it as a backing track for a photo montage I'd made to mark Mum and Dad's twenty-fifth wedding anniversary; the anniversary they never had because Dad died eight months before. Mum's brother had also suggested we might consider playing a song called 'Pamela' for a bit of fun. It was a song that was around long before I was born. I shared the idea with Mum, expecting her to say, 'Oh I remember that.' She did indeed remember but instead she groaned, 'I hated that song!'

With a big swipe of the pen I crossed the suggestion off my list. 'That's the end of that one. Now, are you sure you don't want to leave your wedding ring on?'

There was no contemplation. 'Absolutely not! It will melt and then be no good to anyone.'

I gave her a gentle dig about choosing to bury Dad with his St Christopher's medal. Dad had never worn a wedding ring. He didn't like rings; instead on their wedding day Mum had given him a gold medal of St Christopher. He wore it every day on a long chain but it was never visible. When he died I had voiced the opinion that Mum should keep the medal for herself and eventually for us.

'No!' she'd said. 'It's his, I want him to have it.'

As we got out of the car to go into the chapel of the funeral home to view Dad, Mum dropped the medal and it had fallen into a shallow drain. The tense moment of going to see our dead father vanished for a moment as we all gathered around the drain, staring at the medal shining underneath the metal grid.

'Are you kidding me?' said one brother.

'What are the chances?' said another.

'That's a sign if I ever saw one,' I had declared to Mum. 'You're not supposed to bury it with Dad.' But she did, once we fished it out.

Mum smiled as she remembered the drama. 'Yes, well, burying the medal probably wasn't a very good decision, but anyway I am going up in smoke, I don't need anything.'

'OK. Back to my list! You want to be dressed in the white nightie, no make-up, just your wig.'

'No wig,' she added.

'Oh come on, Mum. The wig suits you.'

She was resolute. 'Send my wig to the Breast Cancer Network, ask them to give it to someone who needs it. It's no use to me anymore.'

'Right, well, if you don't care what you look like, what about me? What will I wear?'

The directive was three words. 'Just look beautiful. Have your hair done, look beautiful and don't wear pale lipstick.'

Mum's bold lipsticks were now in the kitchen and by her bed; they were in my bag, Mary-Ann's bag, in the bathroom and by the kettle. They were always within reach and we were constantly reapplying. What candles are to some, lipsticks were to us, shining bright. It made me smile and cry.

Then the idea came to me. 'I am going to ask everyone to wear bright lipstick to the funeral. In fact, I am going to put it in the funeral notice in the newspaper. If your funeral service won't be littered with bright blooms, it will be bursting with bright lips.'

Mum cracked a smile. I knew she was humouring me.

'Are you scared?' I asked.

'No,' she replied. 'I'm worried about leaving all of you but I'm not scared of dying.' And I believed her.

We had covered just about everything on my 'to know' list. It seemed a small triumph against the virtual ticking clock, but as I looked around I was again reminded of how rapidly her life had come to a sudden halt. Where were all the neat boxes labelled with what was what and who was to have what. She had always been a realist, but perhaps not as much as I had thought.

'Gee, Mum, for someone who knew this was coming you've sure got a lot of crap around the house.'

'I know,' she said apologetically. 'I thought I had more time. I planned to have everything sorted and finalised so that there would be little for you to do.'

She was also referring to the garage full of boxes. Stuff that had come from other houses, boxes of unsorted photos that she had intended to put in albums and never did. No points for guessing who was going to be left with the clean-up. What was I going to do with the sum of her lifetime?

When one parent dies the other still needs a home and still wants the accumulated life. When the last parent goes and the children are grown with their own lives and homes, what do you do with everything? Mum offered a solution with two words: 'Chuck it.'

What was I going to do with those very old photos of people I figured must be relatives but had no real idea who they were? What was the point of leaving them in a box to sit in storage? The politically correct answer would be 'to preserve for future generations and those keen to do family trees', though I knew that person was never going to be me. I resigned myself to becoming the custodian of the boxes not because I would one day get around to collating them into albums; no, the truth was that I would feel bad if I 'turfed' them.

She wore Million Dollar Red

To have only one daughter means that there will only be one son-in-law; my mother chose hers wisely.

Michael didn't have me at 'hello', but the words 'mothers are sacred' early in the piece certainly went in his favour. From day one he knew and respected the relationship I had with Mum largely because he had loved and lost his own. He was also smart enough to read the unwritten signs: if he didn't have my mum on side there was no chance of having me by his. He certainly gave her the works during our courtship of fourteen months and duly took her to lunch and asked for my hand.

'He's a good man and he loves you, that's enough for me,' she'd said, even though my brothers had been doubtful. On our wedding day, unbeknown to me, they had all taken a secret bet on how long our marriage would last. The longest any of them gave us was seven years.

'What would they know? Mother knows best,' laughed Mum when we celebrated our tenth wedding anniversary. Most years Michael would quietly consult Mum on an anniversary gift idea, though there were clearly some years where he failed to do so and other years he had not heeded her advice, and the results were usually disastrous.

Theirs was a relationship of mutual respect. He never commented on how much time we spent together or how often she was at our house. Once we had children she had an open invitation on our family holidays but rarely accepted. Mum was mindful of not overstepping the mark or outstaying her welcome. Whenever we went away on holiday we would return home to an empty house but the lights would be on and there was fresh milk, fresh bread and a casserole on slow in the oven. We knew Nana had been.

I'm sure there were many times over the years that Michael had thoughts he wisely kept to himself, and Mum was quite good at biting her tongue too. My husband truly appreciated the close relationship Mum and I had but every now and then he would voice his concern at how I'd be affected when she was no longer around. I used to shake my head at the unimaginable thought and he'd joke, 'I'll just pop you in a straitjacket.' Now that day was looming and I could feel his unease, anticipating the crash. He'd rung everyone he knew that might have been able to get Mum on a cancer trial in the hope of a miracle, but also accepted way before the rest of us that it was futile. Knowing how important it would be to have her live nearby he found the townhouse and had rallied my brother to make the move happen.

The place we were all gathered, the one that was at the end of our street, had been Mum's home for less than a year but it had made such an incredible and wonderful difference to her final months. It was a gesture never lost on Mum and it changed everything for the better. In those final days he was there when needed but knowing it was more about her children and probably also as a self-protective mechanism he kept an arm's-length distance.

It was early Sunday evening when the only son-in-law in our family went to her side in the cosy nook she had created. 'You look a million bucks, Nana, the jungle juice must be working, they'd written you off.'

Mum managed a smile. 'Hello, Michael.'

I can't recall the other small items of 'weather talk', all I remember was their final few words.

'Well, Nana, you know I'm only here because of you.' He was referring to his place in the family.

To which Mum replied, 'And I am only here because of you.'

I felt my throat tighten as the heartfelt moment lingered. He kissed her on the head, and using all he had to hold his emotions in check he left. We all knew that was code for 'goodbye'.

Later that evening Mum and I were alone sitting in a comfortable moment of silence when a somewhat random thought came to me. 'Will you go looking for Dad?'

I didn't know exactly what I meant by asking such a question. Part of me was holding onto imagery from my childhood belief that after death we're reunited with loved ones among the white fluffy clouds in heaven. The adult, somewhat jaded part of me finds it hard to grasp how that all actually happens. If there is an afterlife do you stay the age you were at the time of your death? And if that's so, why would a man who died in his early fifties want to be reunited with his wife, who was now much older. They were bizarre, irrational thoughts, all of which left more questions than answers. Regardless,

I was interested in whether Mum was looking forward to a reunion with my father.

'No,' she said gently.

It wasn't that I had delusions of two halves waiting to become one again but I assumed there would be an urge or curiosity to find comfort and familiarity with the man she had been married to for almost twenty-five years and had four children with. Perhaps they were not what you would describe as having been 'madly in love', but what exactly does that mean after so long? They'd been best friends.

For most of two decades of their married life they had assumed traditional roles, and it worked. She had been the 'good wife'. We never heard her moan or vent any frustrations at what must have felt like being a solo parent and as a result it rarely bothered us. We didn't know any different and she made it seem perfectly normal. 'Your father works very hard,' she would remind us if we ever whinged that he wasn't home or at concerts or other activities other dads were around for. There must have been countless arguments over the allocation of his time and money – Dad did like to bet on the horses – but apart from the odd argument, and Dad's booming voice was standard anyway, such discussions were never had in our presence.

'Do you remember that photo of us with the homemade hats?' I asked Mum.

She shook her head, clueless as to what I was talking about. It was an image etched in my happy memories, a photo that showed my brothers and me around the age of five, all freshly bathed, dressed in our pyjamas, surrounding my father on his birthday. He would have just arrived home from work. We were grinning from ear to ear, sparklers in hand, the soft glow of candles gently lighting the family huddle, wearing birthday hats made from newspaper.

Mum smiled as I painted the scene but at the same time, and for the first time, I saw the bigger picture through my adult eyes. It was a rented house, my brothers slept in the laundry, we would have seen Dad for thirty minutes before we had to go to bed, and Mum had made the hats out of necessity as she was probably time poor. Mum wasn't even in the happy snap, she was the one taking it, and yet that moment and so many other favourite memories only existed because of her and all she did behind those scenes, each and every day. I know my father was very proud of the homemaker Mum was but I doubt he ever had a true appreciation of what actually went into keeping our family life running smoothly because he never had to worry about it. I wanted to cry tears of belated admiration.

In the later years of their marriage there had been a shift as Mum evolved into a businesswoman. What started as a part-time hobby became very much the principal income. It was a reversal she had revelled in but one Dad had found hard to cope with.

'I wouldn't change anything of what we had, but too much time has passed, I am different now.' The fact was, Mum had been a widow for almost as long as she had been married. There was no bitterness, no anger. It was a state of neutral; she had simply moved on.

My brothers and I were all staying close. The rotation of sleeping over at Mum's had initially been about providing practical care but then shifted to all of us wanting optimal chance of being at Mum's side when she took her last breath.

The result that night was a family sleepover and again the nostalgia wasn't lost. I looked around at my three protective adult brothers and mused how I had spent my younger years wishing for a sister. The fourth child in our family was clearly unplanned but my ten-year-old self had held high hopes that it would correct the gender imbalance of having two brothers. I cried a river when it didn't. We had been fairly typical siblings and enjoyed many happy hours playing tag and swinging on the clothesline, but we also had our fair share of squabbles. My father's nickname for me had been 'Bella da goose', but during a sibling spat Robert and Stephen would call me 'Miss Piggy', in reference to the pink and pudgy pig from *The Muppet Show*, and my round pre-teen and adolescent shape. I remember my anger and tears every time they would say it but I was no pushover and gave as good as I got by hissing back their nicknames, 'Roberto' and 'Stevonovitch', which they hated. Sometimes it would end in a physical scuffle, a cork to the thigh, a Chinese burn; a punch to the arm was possible but never in the stomach, a punch to the stomach was off limits. It made me laugh to remember my mother yelling from the kitchen, 'Your sister won't be able to have babies if you punch her in the stomach,' and the line was never crossed.

That night as I crawled into bed alongside Mum, and my three brothers, now grown men with wives and families of their own, took up positions on the couch and in makeshift beds, it was as if we were back to where we started: a mother and her children. The romance of coming full circle again had me thinking in clichés. Maybe that's what Mum had been waiting for, I thought. Maybe tonight she will slip away.

She wore Mirrored Mauve

Palliative care was scheduled for early morning, and the kind male nurse we had met six months before was on duty. It all seemed so long ago that we'd first sat in the kitchen drinking tea with him when the need for palliative care seemed so far away.

He went through the list of medications and began to cross out many of them. 'You can stop giving these now.'

I guessed that his experience told him that the plethora of the pills was now pointless.

'I'm going to reduce the dose of dexamethasone,' he said. There was no mistaking that he wasn't asking whether we wanted to reduce it, he was telling us.

I let out a big sigh, signalling my resignation, but it ultimately it wasn't my call.

'Mum, the nurse is going to reduce the dexamethasone, do you know what that means?

'Yes.'

'Are you OK with that, Mum? It has to be your decision.'

'Yes.'

It was code for, 'I'm done. I'm now ready to die.'

We had all understood that the express train to the end of the proverbial line was imminent but suddenly it had arrived. A train analogy of all things. There are so many routes that can be taken to end up at the same destination. You choose one and hop on; all the stops are clearly marked but 'Murphy's Law'; when you least expect it, there will be a change in the schedule that no one told you about or you failed to notice, and before you know it you've missed your stop, or the train is holding you captive as it screams past the one you wanted and you have no choice but to accept that it's part of the journey.

The decision I faced was whether I would go along for Mum's ride or sit solo on the platform of hope.

Perhaps it was because I knew deep down that it was what she really wanted. She had given it her very best shot, we had done everything we could. I didn't want her to go, but I didn't want her to remain like she was. There was no point in dragging it out any longer; it would be selfish to ask her to 'stay'. It was another of those 'you don't know until you know' moments. All aboard!

We knew things would move quickly with the withdrawal of the dexamethasone, but just how quickly was a guessing game, and 'quickly' was Mum's priority.

'Mum, they will only increase your level of drugs if you're in pain. If you're not in pain they will not increase the drugs. Do you understand?'

Her gaze met mine. 'Yes.'

The day passed slowly. Mum slept for most of it. She didn't want food or drink or jungle juice for miracles, nothing but ice for her to wet her mouth. In the afternoon I took baby James down to sit on her bed; she opened her eyes and smiled. 'Here is my joy boy.' He did his little bum shuffle dance and bent over to touch her lips as she nodded off again.

I knew her body was taking over, she would never have shut her eyes to a single movement or word of her grandchildren's, but she was exhausted. I was exhausted too. I lay my head just below her chest and cried. I felt her hand on my head and again I was overwhelmed with a mix of raw pain and comfort.

'It will get easier!' she said.

'No it won't!' I sobbed, as she began to stroke my hair.

'You'll never get over it but the sad days will gradually become less. I promise.'

I took no comfort from what she was saying but I was comforted simply by the fact she could still speak, she was still with me, just.

I had brought down a few dresses I had wanted to show her, as we somehow seemed to be 'previewing' her funeral. Mum's brief of 'just look beautiful' was causing me angst. What I thought was beautiful and what she thought was beautiful would often be the same but sometimes radically different. I held up a knee-length olive-green dress with a black print that I'd bought for a function I was supposed to have gone to that week. 'That's lovely but you'll freeze,' she said.

'Don't worry, I can wear your black spencer with the low neck so you won't see it and I'll wear opaque tights.'

We decided on outfits for the girls: pretty skirts that she'd made for them earlier that year, summer twirling skirts.

'But it's winter, they will be cold too, make sure you have tights and jackets to keep them warm.' Mum hated being cold.

With the funeral attire sorted, another item was crossed off my list.

My brothers had been floating in and out throughout the day but as night fell our flock came together. Jayne called in after dinner to check on everyone and I asked her for the hundredth time, 'How long do you think?'

She placed her hand on my arm. 'I think we're close.'

The boys were in the lounge and continued to liberally pour the red wine and paw through old photos retrieved from boxes in the garage. Mary-Ann was going to stay for Mum's wakeful period, but the window of opportunity that had been opening around eight pm for the past few nights failed to eventuate, and she went home. We wondered whether we'd actually had our last conversation with Mum.

I sat in her room watching and waiting for any sign of her waking when I remembered the missing pieces of jewellery. She was the only one who would know where they could possibly be, if indeed she could remember. I needed to ask her but she continued to sleep. I walked over to the couch, got down on my hands and knees and retrieved the boxes from the hiding spot. The four shallow burgundy leather containers were identical. I opened one at a time and again perused the different pieces and completed a visual audit, checking that all was as it should be. Inside the last box were the aquamarine ring and pendant that I'm certain had been missing the day before. How could I have possibly overlooked them?

It was a mystery I would have given more thought to if not for the sound of the doorbell. No one had rung it in days; there had been no surprise visitors. Anyone who was supposed to be there had merely walked in.

The man standing at the door had a special delivery: an empty coffin. Whilst it had felt strange and out of the ordinary to have my mother's 'box' delivered to her garage when she was still alive, it made perfect sense. It wasn't as if things were going to change; there would be no last-minute miracle. Mum didn't want to prolong the grief after her passing, especially not in the form of a delayed funeral. There would be enough to do, and this way there was one less thing.

Steve and I stood at the opened door of the garage in the cold darkness as the hearse backed up the driveway. The late hour offered a veil of discretion and protection from starting a neighbourhood rumour that poor Pam must have died. We could just make out the strikingly plain box as it was removed from the back and lifted to a trestle table in the garage where the white fluorescent light placed a harsh focus on its sole purpose. It was hard to grasp that our mother, who was just a few metres away, would very soon be lying in that box.

Then we spotted it! In the bottom left corner. 'Is that a dent?' Steve said. We couldn't help but chuckle at the unlikely scenario of a defective coffin.

'Do you think it really matters?' I asked.

'Probably not. I don't know why' – scrunching his face – 'but it sort of does.'

We had spent much of the last few days prioritising what truly mattered and trying not to sweat the small stuff. Somehow this seemingly insignificant observation felt important.

Once we pointed out the imperfection to the gentleman from the funeral home he was most apologetic and insisted on taking it back. We watched as the box was slid back into the hearse and pondered the confusion that would occur if anybody saw a hearse coming to the house two nights in a row.

I gave quiet thanks and exhaled with relief when Mum stirred around ten pm.

'You had me worried there for a while, Mum.'

I told her I'd found the missing pieces of jewellery, and with sleepy eyes but a Cheshire Cat smile she asked in a rhetorical tone, 'And where were they?'

Why are mothers always right? That book on parenthood must come with an endless supply of vouchers for being right, I just didn't seem to have found mine yet.

I giggled a little as I told her about the dented coffin, thinking she'd appreciate the irony, but she only mustered a small smile. I couldn't decide whether it was a lack of energy or if her looming fate had begun to diminish her resolve; either way I felt awkward.

I assumed my position of sitting down with my pen and notepad. 'How do I look after the orchid?' There was a magnificent Cymbidium orchid she'd nurtured for almost fifteen years. Every year it had grown more beautiful and rewarded her care with majestic yellow flowers that had a green tinge and red specks, and I didn't want to kill it. I knew I could easily get instruction from any good gardener or even Google but it wouldn't be the same, I wanted my mother's knowledge and tips.

'Don't overwater it. Forget about it in the winter and it will bloom each spring and summer.' Easy for her to say!

It was then I had another idea that I immediately shared with her. 'You are synonymous with flowers and we are on the cusp of spring. Why don't we hand out a bulb wrapped in pretty tulle to everyone at the funeral? They can plant them and they will bloom at this time every year. It will remind everyone of you. What do you think?'

'No one will plant them.'

'Of course they will. Tell me what flower to choose.'

We went through the list of possible contenders. It had to be one that required minimal care and no 'green thumbs'. A set-and-forget flower.

'Daffodils are the easiest,' she offered.

'I was thinking of something a little more elegant, like a tulip.'

'Too hard.'

I tried to think. 'What about a hyacinth? Such a beautiful perfume.'

'No, still too hard.' We workshopped a few more and arrived back at where we started. If I was going to run with the bulb idea it had to be a daffodil. The greater challenge would be to find enough bulbs, because for daffodils to bloom in spring they need to be planted in May. It was August! Most would already be in the ground.

I sent an SMS message to a lifelong friend. Like so many others she had given a genuine open-ended offer of help, asking me to let them know if there was anything they could do. 'I need two hundred daffodil bulbs.' The reply was immediate: 'I'm on it.'

As fatigue exercised dominance again I knew we were done for the night. I walked over to turn off the bedside lamp and cast an eye over Mum to check she was comfortable. My gaze stopped at her hands, which were clasped loosely across her stomach. Something was amiss.

'Mum, where is your wedding ring?' It wasn't unusual for her to take it off when her arthritis flared, but it wasn't by her bed and it certainly wasn't in the inventory of jewellery I had made. I raised my voice to rouse her. 'Mum, where is your wedding ring? It's not in the boxes.'

Without even opening her eyes she responded, 'No. It's under the lamp on the bench,' pointing to the cabinet at the end of the room. I walked over to the lamp and tilted it; under the hollow base was the white gold band. I had to laugh. 'Seriously, Mum, what made you hide it there and when did you think you might let me know?'

'I just told you.'

It's true that a thief was unlikely to have discovered it, but it was almost certain I never would have either! I could envisage the mild panic if she'd passed away with that secret. Yes, a removalist might have seen it months later, but the period in between would have given me night sweats.

I retrieved the ring and walked over to place it on her finger. She hated her hands: chronic childhood eczema had left them wrinkled and badly scarred. From a young age I always felt sad that her memory as a little girl in primary school was that classmates would never hold her hand because they said hers were ugly. Her whole life she remained very conscious of them and it made her an admirer of those who had pretty hands.

'You have beautiful hands,' she used to say to me. The irony was that they were a mirror image of hers minus the scars and thirty years. The marks made no difference to me whatsoever; those hands had made me feel safe and loved. Her hands were creative, they were the tools of her trade. It was with those hands she had made exquisite flower arrangements and wedding bouquets that had brought joy to so many.

I remembered a night years before when the two of us had sipped drinks and eaten fish 'n' chips in the workroom of Flowers by Pamela after it had closed for the day. The familiar tunes of her favourite radio station were playing in the background and I watched in awe and felt enormous pride whilst she created the most significant bouquet of her career: mine. It was a mass of white gardenias and rare exotic white lilies. The fragrance was intoxicating and amongst the blooms she had placed one of my father's cufflinks to symbolize 'something old'. We chatted about how Dad would have been looking forward to his father-of-the-bride duties for his only daughter. Mum even made an extra gardenia buttonhole, and later that night we scaled the fence of the closed cemetery to place it on his grave. We laughed as we scurried back over the fence when we heard the sound of barking dogs that may or may not have been in pursuit of us. I had slept next to Mum on the night before my wedding, and the day with Mum and my two bridesmaids leading into the evening ceremony had been incredibly relaxed and was filled with laughter and joy. In my father's absence Mum had walked me down the aisle, but the truth is I would have had her by my side regardless.

I stood looking at her hardworking hands that were now still. Mum was right, they weren't pretty but they were pretty amazing. The wedding ring was now too big for her fingers, but as I slipped it over her knuckle her hands looked as they always had to me.

The nights had begun to make me feel uneasy because for no logical reason I felt darkness was more likely to snatch my mother's last breath. As I lay next to her it was evident that her level of discomfort had increased. In the early hours of the morning I couldn't sleep and listened to her every breath, struggling with the concept that it was my mother who was dying. Occasionally she stirred and groaned in pain. I went to the kitchen to retrieve the new list of increased medication. At frequent intervals throughout the night I was on the phone to palliative care, who were unwavering in their support and instilled confidence as they talked me through how to 'draw up' needles to inject and give Mum relief.

When it was quiet once more I had begun to fall into a light doze when Mum's voice pulled me back.

'I'm still here aren't I?'

Seriously, when did my mother become so dry? 'Yes, Mum, you are.'

There was another pause. 'It's not going fast enough.' Hearing those words reinforced that she was ready to go and it overrode any of my needs. Mum's position on having the right to die had never faltered over the years, but we weren't cowboys, I wasn't about to do anything illegal. Even so I felt a pang of guilt that my best efforts were not helping.

'I'm doing all I can, Mum.'

She wore Gold Mist Bronze

I t's another day,' Mum moaned, as dawn broke the darkness. Her disappointment was unconcealed; this wasn't living, she was merely existing. We had made it through another night together but I was shattered.

Just after six amt my brother Mick woke and he kept watch over Mum whilst I pinched one of her sleeping pills, broke it in two and swallowed half. Mum had frequently cautioned to only ever take half. I fell into the bed in the sewing room, set the alarm for three hours later and promptly passed out before the pill even had time to work.

When the alarm went off I had to force myself to wake. I felt like I had a hangover but without the luxury of a fun night preceding it. I lay for a few minutes looking around the room in an attempt to clear the haze in my head. I glanced at the back wall, which was lined with large clear plastic storage boxes full of bright materials. On top of one was a striped cardboard box that looked familiar but I couldn't think why. Curiosity got the better of me and I got up and opened it. Underneath layers of white tissue paper was my First Communion dress. From the moment the grandchildren arrived, one of the first challenges Mum had set herself was to convert the little white dress into a christening gown. She had soaked it in Napisan for two days to restore it to a perfect white. After each of my children's baptisms she had sent it off to have their name embroidered in white on the inside hem. To think I had teased her about not having kept my baby singlets and crib. I was holding a true keepsake, one that I could hand down to my children. My eyes filled like puddles as I folded up the gown and put it back in its box. I glanced in on Mum, saw that she was sleeping and made my way into the kitchen. Mare had arrived whilst I slept and was pouring a cup of tea.

'How are you feeling, darling? The boys said you had a rough night. Tea? Pammie's GP has just rung. She wanted you to know that she is back in town and is happy to offer any assistance at all. She has left her numbers for you.'

The call reminded me that the GP's return was one of the reasons Mum had declared that she was going to die on Tuesday. It was also the day her oncologist Dr John was back from annual leave, even though there was no plan to see him again. If Mum was right, then it was D-day. It would be the last day for the rest of my life that I would spend with my mother. It was a strange sensation and despite knowing her quality of life was now gone I was hoping her mind couldn't be that powerful.

I rang the GP to take up her offer of assistance and her arrival coincided with the visit from palliative care. Together they decided that it would be best to set up a syringe driver, which would automatically administer pain relief into the bloodstream through an intravenous needle. All of a sudden I was relieved of my nursing duties. I felt useless. It was certainly a lot easier than dishing out multiple injections and pills that Mum was having trouble swallowing, but it was another marker of doom and my interpretation was that we could only be hours from the finishing line.

'Will you be back at the same time tomorrow?' the GP asked the male nurse as he walked to the door.

'Surely not!' I interjected.

With sincerity and kindness he replied, 'With a bit of luck, no.'

Mary-Ann and Jayne prepared the towels to give Mum a Turkish bath. 'She really enjoys the hot towels, it's very soothing,' Mare said. The two of them had the procedure down pat whereas I found the smell of the sweet cleansing solution overwhelming. I left them to it knowing Mum was in the safest hands.

I was startled by the screams of pain that came from the bedroom a few minutes later and ran in. Jayne's nursing background allowed her quickly to realise the pain was caused by the catheter that had dislodged. She knew how to remove it and Mum's distressing cries ceased immediately.

'Thank God you're here, Jayne,' I said. 'We wouldn't have had a clue what was wrong.'

'It's OK, Pammie. It's OK,' said Mare, stroking her sister's brow, but there was no response from Mum. They dressed her in a fresh nightgown and Mum was calm once more.

The room was very quiet. It was so quiet that above the murmur of the machine that automatically dispensed the medication into Mum's bloodstream, I could hear the soft music coming from the radio that was on in the kitchen. Watching Mum as she slept, I could see that she was peaceful and that the higher dose of pain relief was having the desired effect. I waited patiently for her wakeful period, even though I knew it would be short.

The hours went by but Mum didn't stir. It hadn't occurred to me that stronger medication would reduce her level of communication to nil. I turned to Jayne for reassurance that there was still time for last words.

'I don't think so, Kel, but she can hear you, she can absolutely hear you.'

'What a fucking idiot,' I muttered to myself as a rapid internal conversation began. I'd been with her every minute and I'd still missed her last words. Well, I hadn't actually missed them, I just hadn't known at the time that they were her last words. Why didn't I take the opportunity to exchange poignant words before they increased the painkillers? I tried to recall her last words, even if they weren't significant. I couldn't remember them.

'Do you remember Mum's last words?' I asked Mare.

'No, darling, I don't.'

How could I mark down Mum's last words if I couldn't remember what they were? Already I was feeling robbed.

'You know what Mum would say, don't you?' said Mare. '"It doesn't matter." And it doesn't matter, Kel. Come on, where is the lipstick? Put some on. I will too.'

We reapplied bright lipstick throughout the day, more than was necessary, but it was comforting. I rang my brothers to tell them to stay close. We were on high alert, looking for any signs that would indicate the last few minutes.

'You will know,' Jayne said. 'Her breathing will change. You will know.'

How will I know? I thought. That's like when someone hands you a newborn baby and says, 'You will know the different cries. The cry that says I'm hungry, the cry that says I'm tired.' Really? Perhaps I wasn't born with that intuition, all I ever heard was noise, and it all sounded the same to me. What if I didn't notice the change in Mum's breathing?

Reason told me that despite every effort and watchful eyes I could still end up missing 'the' moment. I knew I would get over it if I did, what choice would I have? But it wouldn't stop me worrying about it.

The build-up was stressful. Just because I was witnessing the slow winding down of my mother's body didn't necessarily mean it would be a steady countdown. There was no guarantee of a textbook sequence, it could just end with no warning. I knew it had to be soon: Mum was ready, the funeral was organised, her family was close, she'd said her goodbyes. All the important things were in order and she was giving her body permission to rest. Her fight was over, it was time to let go.

The afternoon slipped away with little change as the family gathered. Wine was poured, lipstick applied.

At dusk Nana's new perfect box was delivered. I stood in the garage alone, looking at the plain coffin, but forced myself to retreat from the broken feeling that threatened to overwhelm me and went inside.

The holding pattern continued as Mum's breathing remained calm and steady. The consumption of wine continued too, with a homemade curry from Jayne that the brothers gratefully received, but the conversation was in hushed tones. I had no appetite so decided to drop home and check on the children.

I went into Mum's room, where Jayne was keeping watch whilst the boys ate. I held Mum's hand and found myself talking in a loud voice as if somehow I would be able to stir her. 'Mum, I'm going home to put the kids to bed. I'll be back in around thirty minutes.' I was taken aback when her eyes appeared to flicker. Does it mean something? I thought. Did she understand me and was trying to communicate that she understood? 'Mum, if you understand me, do it again, flick your eyelids again.' And she did. 'Bloody hell, you can understand me! Down but not out.'

A wave of reassurance washed over me. I looked at the clock beside her bed, which read 7.25 pm. It didn't look like she was going to meet her Tuesday deadline; we would have her for another day. Mum then began to make small groaning sounds. I turned to Mary-Ann and Jayne for possible decoding of what the sounds meant but neither knew. 'I'm going to go now, Mum. See you soon.' And again she fell silent.

I arrived home to see four happy, freshly bathed children still up watching television. They were dressed in the bright pyjamas that had been custom-made by Nana. They looked angelic.

'How is Nana?' asked McKenzie with concern but not fear.

'She is sleeping, she's very tired,' I replied and sat down next to them. We talked about their school day, what they'd had for dinner and other non-pressing matters. Michael looked at me and said nothing but I knew what his eyes were asking. 'We are close,' I said.

We started the process of putting the children to bed and as I tucked James into his cot and sat on each child's bed I repeated the words, 'Baby Jesus, meek and mild, please look after my darling child.' They smiled even though it meant nothing to them. Why would it? It was but a sentimental moment repeating the line delivered to my brothers and me every night of my childhood by our mother.

'Make sure you give Nana a kiss from me,' yelled Sidney from the room she shared with Stella, which prompted her sister to demand the same. I had begun to make my way downstairs when McKenzie called me back to her room. I stuck my head back in through the doorway.

'Tell Nana that we are wearing the pyjamas that she made for us.'

'I will, darling'.

It was just after eight pm when I walked back into Mum's house. My sisters-in-law Vink and Haillie had arrived, Jayne and Mare were still there and everyone but Mick was in the lounge room.

'Hi,' I called out from the doorway but walked straight in to Mum.

Mick was keeping watch and massaging her feet. I kissed Mum on the forehead. 'I'm back, Mum. The girls want you to know that they're wearing their new pyjamas.' I sat on the side of the bed and held her hand; my brother continued to massage her feet; neither of us said anything. It was quiet but for the gentle hum of the medical driver administering the intravenous pain relief.

Only a few minutes had passed when I saw Mum had opened her eyes. She wasn't looking at me, she was looking upward, but without focus, like a vacant stare. I nudged my brother. 'Look!' We were both looking at her looking at nothing when I realised that it must be a sign. Instantly I knew. I yelled without taking my eyes off her, 'Robert, Stephen! Come quickly.' They ran in, everyone did.

Robert and Stephen joined Mick and me at Mum's bedside and the family circle became complete. In a split second her breathing began to change. The calm rhythm moved to random short breaths. It wasn't as dramatic as I had expected but there was no mistaking that it was the change we had been watching for. Steve leant over and gently closed his mother's eyes.

'Go, Mum! Go!' I whispered. 'Fly.'

We were willing her to go and with a mixture of silent tears and pride we watched as she took her final few breaths.

'Thank you, Mum. Thank you. Now go.' And she did.

She wore Wine With Everything

It was quiet once more. I looked to the clock that read August 17th, 8.22 pm. I looked over my shoulder to everyone in the room and smiled. 'She did it! She said she would die on Tuesday.' I turned around again and looked at Mum. Of course she did, I thought. How did I ever doubt her?

We were riding a euphoric wave; the adrenaline was pumping through me. I was able to fulfil my promise to Mum to be there for her last breath. Better still, all her children were. We did it! It was perfect. Within a few minutes we were all reflecting on Mum's final moments; we could not ever have imagined a more beautiful end.

Robert sent a text message to his wife Sharon. 'She's gone,' was all it said.

I called my husband. 'Nana's gone.' There was silence. I suggested he ring our neighbour and take up her offer to watch over the kids whilst he came down to say goodbye.

In a nurturing but hardly practical move I pulled the blanket up to her waist and held one of her hands in mine. I had no reason to let go; I wanted to see it through to the very end until it was time for her to physically leave. But when would it be time?

'Bring the wine in,' said Steve, and we filled our glasses and continued to marvel at Mum's last few moments.

The whirring sound of the medical driver that was no longer needed had no place in the tranquil moment and I leant over to turn it off. The switch was within the clear Perspex casing, which was locked, so I turned it off at the power point. Had I thought it through for a moment I would have realised that there is a very good reason why such devices require more than a simple flick of a switch, which explained why my action immediately set off a loud alarm. 'So much for the peaceful moment,' I cursed.

I rang palliative care to advise them Mum had died and confessed to trying to shut down the driver. Within fifteen minutes a nurse arrived. She turned off the alarm, removed the catheter and all other signs of medical assistance.

'What time would you like me to arrange for the undertakers to come?' she asked.

'Midnight, I think.' Midnight felt symbolic. It would mean I would see my job through until literally the end of the last day Mum was alive.

The nurse looked at her watch and clearly did a quick mental calculation that midnight was three and a half hours away. 'I think perhaps that might be a little too long,' she said with a knowing tone. 'Over the next few hours her body will start to change.'

'You mean rigor mortis?' I said.

'Yes.'

I knew that was an image of my mother that I did not want to be left with.

'How about eleven pm?' she suggested.

The real countdown had begun and I felt a shiver ripple through my body.

The next call was to the priest. I was tempted not to given our last meeting but Mum had decided against finding another priest so I figured I should ring him.

'I'm sorry to call you so late, Father, but my mother has just passed away.'

'No, not at all. I will come right away,' he said.

It must have only been ten minutes later that he knocked on the door.

'Hello, Father, thank you for coming.'

He smiled and we walked into Mum's room, where the family was still gathered, and he delivered a final blessing – a ritual that was short but moving and felt fitting. At the conclusion the priest made the sign of the cross over Mum. 'In the name of the Father, the Son and the Holy Spirit.' We all joined in making the sign of the cross. The priest then placed his hand on her head

'May your soul rest in peace, Pat.'

Within a split second Steve and I had locked eyes with each other in a silent scream: 'Pat?' Another calm moment had evaporated. 'Who the hell is Pat?' I said under my breath. 'Her name is Pam!'

The outrageous mistake suddenly seemed amusing. I could see my brothers thinking the same and I dared not look at anyone else in the room as I feared I would start to laugh. Normally our family wouldn't hold back but given that no one said anything it was clear that the non-verbal consensus was to let it go.

'Thank you, Father, that was very nice,' said Steve. 'Can I offer you a drink? A wine? A beer? A tea?' To our surprise he accepted. 'I'll have a beer.'

Steve, who is happy to drink with anyone, went to grab the beers, and my brothers and I moved to the lounge and engaged in a friendly, informal chat about when the funeral would be. I expressed Mum's wishes not to delay the inevitable.

'Mum was very clear that she didn't want to prolong this process – we would like the funeral as soon as possible.'

'It's already a very busy week,' the priest said. 'We will need to coordinate with the funeral director and see what we can do.'

Steve and I walked the priest to the door but as soon as he was gone we released the laughter we'd all been holding in for half an hour. 'Yes, see you later, Father Bob,' joked Steve.

'Well I'm glad Pat has gone to heaven,' I pitched in, 'but where the hell does that leave Mum?'

We all shook our heads at the absurdity and black humour, grabbed the glasses of red and went back to sit with Mum.

We continued to rehash her perfect final moments. Was it luck or did she choose when to let go? I was convinced it was the latter. 'I'm telling you. I told her that I was going to put the kids to bed and she waited until I came back. She waited until we were all here then let go.'

'She really does look so peaceful,' someone said, and we all agreed. I would never have expected a death afterglow and yet that's what we appeared to be basking in. We felt liberated from the fear of death, victorious even.

Mum would have been so proud of us. I was proud of us. We were amazing!

I sat holding Mum's cool hand and my eye caught her wedding band. I knew she wanted me to have it because it was one of the many questions I had asked. I placed my hand down on the blanket in front of hers, connected the tips of our ring fingers and in a seamless transfer slid the band across. My inner voice didn't declare 'I will never take this off!' for whilst it would have sounded poetic it was unrealistic. My internal chatterbox instead observed how the thick white-gold band looked against my thin yellow-gold wedding band. That looks crap! I thought. Oh well, bad luck, it's staying there.

I felt a firm hand on my shoulder and a kiss on the top of my head. I looked up to see that it was my husband. One of my brothers handed him a glass of red and he listened to us recount again how empowering Mum's last seconds were. Despite our upbeat mood, Michael remained reserved and his expression showed his concern for how it was all going to play out once the reality set in. He emptied his glass and gave Mum one last kiss on the forehead. 'Goodbye, Nana,' he said and left.

I have no idea what else we did or talked about in the few hours that followed but they seemed to vanish and I felt a knot in my stomach when the doorbell rang.

Two gentle giants stood outside. Even though we had been expecting the undertakers we were never going to be ready. They must be well used to people needing another final few moments with a loved one, and stood patiently at the door.

I went back in to Mum, still trying to grasp the whole concept of 'last time ever'. This was it. It really was the last of the lasts, said the voice in my head, the absolute end of the line. The euphoria I had felt over her beautiful last breath was gone. I knew I was looking at and touching her for the final time in my life and there was no way to make it last.

The pebbles! The random thought snapped me out of my feelings of helplessness as I remembered the four pebbles, one from each of the children that were to travel with Nana to heaven. I took them from the side table and placed them under her hands. Now she was ready. A potent mix of fear and sadness rose as I gave her one last kiss and told her, 'All is well.' I took a mental picture and left the room.

My brothers and I sat in the lounge and left the undertakers to do their job. More red was poured as we made conversation and pretended not to listen to the clicking of the trolley wheels and the body bag being zipped up. I was glad I didn't physically see it but my senses were witness and the sounds made me nervous and tense. No one moved as we heard the wheels of the trolley that carried my dear mother roll out the front door. The undertakers returned a few minutes later to ask if there were any instructions. I handed over the bag containing the freshly laundered white nightgown, which had been stitched up, and requested that she be dressed in it. 'Oh, and please make sure the pebbles in my mother's hands stay there, her grandchildren want her to take them to heaven.'

They nodded. 'We'll take good care of your mother.' The door closed and we were left feeling empty in a way I had never known.

The last of the red wine was drunk as my brothers and I made attempts to grasp back a little of the united triumph we had shared a few hours before, but we were all exhausted. The reality of our mother's death was already being absorbed in different ways.

'I think we should all stay the night here together,' Steve said.

'I'll take the couch,' said Mick.

'Not me!' said Robert. 'I'm outta here.' He couldn't cope with any more, and without saying another word he walked out into the cold night. Steve and Mick took the couch and the spare bed and without a second thought I crawled into my mother's bed.

As my head sank into the soft pillow and I pulled the duvet up under my chin I could smell her. Despite my lack of sleep I realised that adrenaline and overtiredness gave me slim chance of truly resting. I looked over at the bedside table that had held her concoctions of pills and creams; there would be enough there to last me years. I reached out and grabbed one of the half-used packets, popped one through the seal and broke the little white pill in two. I lay my head down and watched the bedside clock tick over the final minutes of my mother's last day. August 17th 2010. Our new lives would begin in the morning.

She wore Orange Flip

The sound of 'nothing' was deafening. It had been many years since my day had started with anything other than the noise of young children, and the silence in my mother's house announced the reality. The surrounds we had sought comfort in a few hours before had transformed into a brutal declaration that she was gone forever. We all decided to depart for our respective homes and meet again in a few hours.

As I walked into the hallway of my home, our little girls, who had heard the telltale sound of the key opening the front door, were running down the hallway to meet me. Three sets of arms wrapped tightly around my legs and waist. 'Are you OK, Mummy? Are you sad?'

I bent down to kiss them. 'Yes, I am sad but I'm OK and Nana isn't sick anymore, she is now happy in heaven.'

With their grip still firm around my waist we walked into the kitchen, where baby James was propped up in his highchair happily making a mess of his breakfast, and Michael enveloped me in strong bearhug.

'I'm not going to work today,' he said. It was the first and last time I ever heard him utter those words. He went to make tea whilst I sat down for a few minutes to answer the kids' questions.

'Did Nana say anything before she died?' asked Sidney.

'No she didn't,' I replied.

'When she died did she just go—?' She mimicked a movement where her head jolted to the side of her shoulder and her eyes shut tight.

'Well not quite like that because she had been sleeping all day.'

'Did you tell her we were wearing the pyjamas she had made us?' enquired McKenzie.

'I sure did. In fact it was the first thing I said to Nana when I got back to her house after saying goodnight to you, and just a few minutes later she died.'

'What about the pebbles?'

'Don't worry, she has the pebbles, I put them in her hand.'

There were no tears, everyone seemed calm.

'Does that mean you will come home tonight, Mummy?' asked Sidney as she picked up her schoolbag.

'Yes, darling. Nana doesn't need me anymore.'

I showered, grabbed a coffee and headed back to Mum's. As I unlocked the door I could hear the faint sound of the radio playing softly in the kitchen, but as I walked down the hallway loneliness crept up behind me and came crashing down. Mum had been bedridden for more than a week but her half-finished crossword book was still on the coffee table, alongside several Lotto tickets. I picked up the losing ticket; she had written the winning numbers across the top and circled the few that she had. Without warning my body released the same primal sounds that came from McKenzie the day she stood in the street. She was gone. My mother was really gone.

The loud sobs didn't last long and by the time Steve and Mick arrived just a few minutes later my eyes were only on a slow leak.

'Are you all right?' Steve asked, although he knew the answer. Nothing was all right anymore, in fact it was all wrong. Facilitating Mum's good death now seemed like the easy part. Life without her was still unfathomable. Although it was officially our first day without her, we knew from experience after Dad died that our private mourning would be weeks away. The dying was done but there were still many things to do in preparation for the public grieving. I was already feeling grateful and incredibly relieved that the enormity of the tasks ahead felt less daunting because there were no major decisions to make. All I had to do was action Mum's wishes. Whilst I made calls to arrange for the funeral director and priest to return, Steve and Mick looked through Mum's brown leather address book to let her close friends know of her passing.

The next thing on my list of things to do was a death notice. 'What shall we put in the paper?' I asked the boys.

'I don't know, you're the wordsmith,' said Steve, opting out.

'We don't need individual notices, just do one from all of us,' suggested Mick.

Does anyone even read death notices anymore? I knew Mum's generation certainly did, especially as the odds were there would be someone they knew in those columns. I started to feel pressure to write something meaningful but struggled with the thought of trying to condense what our mother meant to us in just a few lines. Damn! I cursed. I'd planned for just about everything but didn't think to ask her what she wanted in her death notice. Then again, I knew it wouldn't have been a priority for her, she would have just said, 'I don't mind, you'll know what to write.'

I sat down and wrote her name across the top of the paper – 'Pamela Mary Curtain' – hoping that it would somehow prompt poetic words to flow. Don't overthink it, I urged the chatter in my head. Keep it simple! Her name was sitting lonely on the page. Underneath it I wrote her date of birth and her date of death; it looked like two bookends. As my eyes welled the words came.

Pamela Mary Curtain
July 6th 1939 – August 17th 2010

Fought the hard fight for her greatest love, her family. The master of beautiful blooms, the best roast, dancing dresses and fairy gardens. Devoted wife of Kevin Joseph (Tosca) (dec). Mother of all mothers to Robert, Kellie, Stephen and Michael. Friend and mother-in-law to Michael, Vink, Sharon and Haillie, and the world's only amazing 'Nana Pana' to McKenzie, Sidney, Matthew, Stella, Emily, Harley, James, Bentley (due Sept) and those still a twinkle in the eye. Thank you, Mum, you were all class. Rest now, all is well.

I rang the paper's classifieds number, read out the snapshot of my mother and gave Mum's credit card details. I guessed that technically I wasn't supposed to be using the credit card of a dead person but Mum had been adamant she wanted to pay for it all.

'Shit, I'm glad we went the group tribute, death notices are bloody expensive,' I said to the boys. I placed a tick next to 'death notice' on my list. The next line read 'casket flowers'.

As I overheard the boys have the same conversation with several people about Mum's death, I picked up the address book, ran my finger down to the tab that said 'F' and turned to the page for all contacts relating to Flowers by Pamela. I called one of the ladies that had worked for Mum for many years. She was shocked and saddened as to how quickly it had all ended. 'I'm so sorry, Kel, is there anything I can do?'

'Actually, there is. Mum had asked if you would do her casket flowers. She wanted a white ring of gardenias just like Princess Diana.'

'Of course. I'd be honoured.'

Another of her ladies also shared a conversation that she'd had with Mum just a few weeks before. 'Pam asked me to make sure the inside of the hearse is full of green ivy, she didn't want the casket to be visible.' The attention to such a small detail was typically Mum but I hadn't realised until that moment that her planning wasn't just about logistics, it was about preparing everyone for her death.

We were dreading our third meeting with the priest but we had Mum's wishes to fulfil and a desire to give her the send-off she deserved. As we sat down to discuss the service it was clear he had a firm formula and it certainly didn't include the Racey hit that Mum and I had joked about.

'No, that's not appropriate,' he said. He went on to explain that people are losing sight of the real purpose of a requiem mass, using examples of families playing football team theme songs. 'A church is not the place and there are now new guidelines and we need to follow them,' the priest said.

I could feel the muscles in my neck start to tense.

'Who will be doing the readings?'

'My aunt will read one and that's all.'

The priest deferred to protocol and insisted there be two. 'Who will be doing the prayers of the faithful?' he enquired.

'No one! We don't want any.'

Once again his set of rules got in the way. 'Your mother told me that she wanted a full mass, there must be at least three prayers of the faithful.'

I was ready to explode! I wanted to pull the pin on the whole thing and go in search of another priest, regardless of my mother's wishes. We needed someone who would allow us to farewell my mother and celebrate her life in a way we saw fit, not according to church protocol.

It was staggering to think that my father's funeral had been held in a Catholic church more than two decades earlier with no fewer than four priests who were up for a laugh and supported anything that unified those who loved him. The eulogy I had written was a limerick that contained the words 'shifty shit', a turn of phrase Dad often used to describe the sly actions of others. Prior to reading it out in church I sought permission to use the mild expletive in a house of God, but the clergy didn't so much as raise an eyebrow to my request and were somewhat amused that I had even asked. Fast forward twenty years and I was stonewalled by a priest who appeared desperate to bring back the old days in the name of political correctness, even if it came at the expense of alienating a depleting flock.

I wasn't listening to much else of what was said; all I could hear was my mother's words loud and clear: 'It doesn't matter.' In the scheme of things none of what was being dictated really mattered but it didn't stop me wanting or trying to break free of the constraints.

The priest left and I immediately vented my frustrations to my brothers, who were also annoyed but not enough to lead or support a defection. I began a new list, which included the roles that would need to be filled for the long, formal church service we didn't want. What readings would we choose? Who would I ask to read them? If I didn't want standard generic prayers of the faithful read out then I would have to write them, and in keeping with the modus operandi I would have to end each one with 'Lord hear us'. Already I could hear the Catholics both lapsed and practising in the congregation respond in monotone: 'Lord hear our prayer.' The whole thing galled me. I was walking around the house like a caged lion; I ended up in Mum's ensuite applying a lipstick: Raisin Rage. Oh the irony, I thought.

In stark contrast, our meeting with Deb the funeral director a short time later was like being wrapped in a warm hug, and I'm certain that was entirely because the big decisions had already been made by Mum at our first meeting, the cardboard box was in the garage ready to be decorated, and all that was left to do was confirm a time and date for the service.

'We need this wrapped up as soon as possible please, Deb, certainly before the weekend. The priest says he is free Friday.'

As we watched her look through her diary we sensed there was a problem. 'I'm afraid we're already fully booked for Friday,' she said apologetically.

It all seemed quite absurd that we had struck a busy week for funerals. 'Is there any way we can make this work? Mum isn't being buried and she wants us to say our last goodbye at the church, no one is going to the crematorium.'

'OK, well I know Pam's sons and son-in-law are the pallbearers so that saves some manpower, but the problem is the funeral cars, we only have so many and you are a big family,' Deb said.

'Oh we don't need funeral cars! We want to drive ourselves to the church. All we need is a hearse for Mum, we can use our cousin's ute if we need to.' We all chuckled.

'Let me see what I can do.'

We sat hopeful as we watched Deb make a phone call. 'OK, Friday morning it is, but a few decisions need to be made quickly. You will need to choose readings and songs so that they can be printed in the funeral booklet.'

I knew Mum wasn't a big wrap for those either. 'No booklet, thanks, we just want a simple card with a picture and a thank-you. I have organised the flowers too.' I expressed my lament at the restrictions that were being imposed by the church denying us the opportunity to play the Racey song to add a little light relief to the solemn occasion.

'I'm sorry,' Deb said. 'We don't have any say over what happens inside a church.'

I'm sure anyone that would have cared to notice would literally have seen the light go on in my head with yet another idea.

I had dreamt a lot of her funeral, of what it would be like, who would come. I dreamt of the eulogy I would give, what to put in it. I knew my heart would ache over her absence at special occasions and major milestones, though already I knew it was the ordinary days without her that would hurt most. When the second morning of the rest of my life without her came I sat down and began to write.

I had loved to write rhyming poems as a kid and into my late teens the subjects were mostly friendship or a boy crush, and my sentiments were relative but in reality puddle deep. Mum and Dad had delighted in my words and I produced several verses for their anniversary or on request for a birthday. The limerick I had penned for my father's eulogy was humorous and I'd also jotted down a rhyme about the little things we would miss. I wanted to pay Mum the same tribute; it would have felt grossly unfair not to. The words that imagined my life without Mum spilled effortlessly onto the paper as if she was talking to me, telling me to acknowledge my sadness and tears but cautioning that life wouldn't stop for them. There would still be washing to be done, kids wanting something, the house to be cleaned, and meals to be cooked. 'That's life,' she would say. To 'stop' wasn't bad; but my life and everyone else's would continue, so I might as well get on with it.

> *Get yourself up, begin the day,*
> *It will start without you anyway.*
> *Let tears fall into the cup of tea,*
> *Then get on with what needs to be.*
> *That loving voice you no longer hear,*
> *Cuddle those babies to feel her near.*
> *It's not what is lost, but what was had,*
> *She prepared you for the good times and bad.*
> *And in a moment alone at day's end,*
> *My heart will break all over again.*
> *Put your lipstick on and start the day,*
> *You know she'd want it to be that way.*

The words felt right but looked bleak on the page. I wanted people to smile when they read the memorial card, even if it was through their tears. It needed a happy backdrop. I turned to my McKenzie, who was sitting beside me. 'Darling, I want you to draw Nana one last picture.'

The children were constantly drawing pictures for Nana, whether it was a quick scribble or a painstaking colourful line drawing. Each one seemed to have a rainbow and Nana had admired them all and kept most of them. Some had even been framed and placed on her mantle.

'What will I draw?' she asked.

Wary of not wanting to place undue pressure on my seven-year-old I gave her a gentle steer but free rein. 'How about a picture of Nana and all her grandchildren?'

With the funeral only forty-eight hours away there was something else that also required an injection of colour: Nana's box! In the late afternoon my brothers, sisters-in-law, Mary-Ann and all the grandchildren gathered in Mum's garage armed with wine, lollies, bright paints and chalk. I hoped that I wasn't going to regret Mum's decision to order a plain recycled cardboard coffin. In theory we were going to transform it into a unique eye-catching piece of art, but I feared the result produced by six preschool children, most of whom were under five, would be a mishmash of smudged colours, objects no one would recognise and cries of 'I want to start again!'

There was nothing warm and fuzzy about the atmosphere when we all came together. It was cold in the garage, the white fluorescent lighting didn't help, and our loud voices echoed harshly. 'We need music!' declared Steve, as he walked inside to get the kitchen radio whilst I retrieved the little blow heater from Mum's ensuite.

The children sat on the ground in one line against the wall, waiting patiently to begin, though no one seemed sure where to start. No one except Mary-Ann. We watched as my aunt swung into teacher mode and effortlessly commanded the children's attention. 'I am going to help you paint or draw anything you want to draw on Nana's box to make it beautiful. Everyone will get a turn but we must do it one at a time. OK?'

'Yeeeees,' the chorus replied.

The mood lifted as a steady stream of Mum's favourite tunes played over the radio, and the little heater and sounds of laughter took the chill off the air. Wine was poured as each one of us took turns to leave a mark around the sides of Nana's box. Over the course of an hour the brown box became a canvas for stick figures, trucks, flowers, stars, cars, love hearts, butterflies and of course rainbows. In shades of blue, green, pink and yellow, we left our handprints and names in a symbolic family chain. Even in the dreams I'd had I could never have imagined such a beautiful expression of family and love. In the past the sight of a coffin had filled me with dread and a feeling of wanting to turn away, yet Mum's coffin was something you wanted to look at. It made my heart sing and break. We had considered that the exercise would take away some of the fear for the children as they tried to process where Nana was during the funeral service, but who would have guessed the therapy it provided for us all.

When everyone had gone I went inside and as I had done each evening since Mum had died I turned on the hall lamp and Mum's bedside light. I didn't want the house to lose its lived-in feeling. Whilst it seemed a little strange I felt compelled to take pictures of Nana's box because I wanted to remember it and all the beautiful detail. More importantly I wanted her grandchildren to remember.

'Wear your bright lipstick!' read the funeral notice in the morning paper. I laughed and wondered whether anyone would take note of the request; Mum certainly hadn't thought so. The list of things to do for the service was almost complete. My brothers had organised the catering and alcohol for the wake, which was to be held in the hall of another local church because ironically the hall of our church of choice wasn't available. 'Just another sign we should have ditched this mob,' I mocked.

I had quickly written a few obligatory lines for the prayers of the faithful for people to read. 'Dear Lord, we give thanks for the beauty of flowers and the arrangements Pam was able to create with them,' or something to that effect. I don't think I even kept a record of them, which showed how insignificant the forced prayers were to us. My brother Mick had written his own eulogy that he wanted to read, all that was left to do was complete my tribute.

There had been so many occasions over the last few days that I had given silent thanks that Mum and I had discussed her wishes for her funeral. Together we had organised just about everything except her eulogy. It was a subject we never discussed and despite wanting to be prepared I could never bring myself to start it before she was gone; to do so somehow didn't feel right.

I sat at my computer, looking at a blank screen. How would I ever do this woman justice? As the words bounced around in my head so did the powerful realisation of just how good she was. Her dry humour in those final days seemed out of character for her. My mother wasn't naturally funny – or was she and we had never noticed nor given her the platform? The comic and spontaneous parent had been Dad, or so we had thought. I suddenly felt sad at having pigeonholed her as the 'non-funny' one and marvelled at her humility at being happy to be in the background while others shone, the steady rudder of our family ship. It was long overdue but it was time to put her in the spotlight.

I knew I was trying too hard to create powerful prose and my frustration increased as the words failed to materialise. When Dad had died we had wanted a meaningful quote to print on the funeral booklet. We had simply opened a little book of meaningful quotes and it had fallen open on one from Pope John Paul II: 'A human being is a single being. Unique and unrepeatable.'

'That's the one! It's perfect,' Mum had said.

'Come on, Mum. Help me out!' I yelled to the empty house as I Googled 'meaningful quotes', desperately searching for a few lines that would encapsulate our mother. Then my mind wandered to a photo that took pride of place on Mum's hall table. It was a picture of Mum and me with McKenzie on her christening day: three generations. I had intended to buy a simple silver frame for the lovely photo but came across one with a quote by Eleanor Roosevelt around the border: 'Yesterday is history, tomorrow mystery, today is a gift.' Slow, heavy tears started to run in a steady stream; tomorrow was indeed a mystery but there was one certainty that every tomorrow would be without my mother. And then the words came.

She wore 24K Orange

It was a beautiful morning for a funeral. The sun was out early and the air felt crisp as I left the house to have my hair blow-waved, as I'd promised Mum I would. A few friends had organised to drop by the house to help dress the children and make the girls' hair pretty. It wasn't the day for their dad to attempt something so ambitious.

We were on a fairly tight schedule and it was all going to plan until the calm turned out to be a prelude to a storm. When I arrived home all the kids were ready bar one.

McKenzie was still in her pyjamas, lying on the couch sobbing, almost delirious with a raging temperature. 'I feel sick, Mummy.'

My instincts told me it wasn't illness but that the day ahead was simply overwhelming her. Regardless there was little point in trying to convince her and I had no choice but to call 'time out'. I took her into our bedroom and let her climb into bed, lay next to her and let her cry. A suggestion was made that someone stay behind with her, but I just couldn't entertain the thought of her missing the service. I called our local doctor, explained our predicament, made it to and from the surgery within thirty minutes and arrived home with medication for an ear infection. So much for the so-called mother's intuition. McKenzie crawled back into our bed and I dashed to put on my make-up, making sure to go heavier on the eyes and apply the brightest lipstick of Mum's I could find. Then as if by some divine intervention McKenzie appeared in my bathroom. 'I'm OK now.'

I helped her put on the blue, red and white flowered twirling skirt that Mum had made in triplicate, and then just as Mum had asked I rugged them all up in the matching red cardigans she had bought. With no time to spare I threw on a spencer and thick black opaque stockings to keep me warm, stepped into my olive-green dress and patent leather heels then piled the kids into the car and raced to the church. We were already ten minutes late. Shit! Mum was always annoyed when I was late. I cursed under my breath.

There wasn't a spare seat or even standing room in the church. It was quiet but for the sound of the church organ playing softly. I could feel my right heel slipping in and out of my shoe as we began walking down the middle aisle. Shit! I thought again, I knew those shoes were a tad too big but they were the ones that looked the best. Bad decision. I saw people clutching the service cards and daffodil bulbs. My old friend had moved heaven and earth to source enough bulbs and the night before had brought together women of the village to share a few wines and conversation whilst they wrapped them in pretty tulle sacs tied with ribbons. I knew could count on her and them.

Mum's beautiful box was at the end of the aisle and on top, just as she had requested, sat the thick ring of gardenias. The rich heavy scent of the perfect delicate white blooms was inescapable as we walked past to sit in the front pews.

'Nana is in the box now?' asked Stella, as if wanting confirmation of what we had said would happen.

'Yes she is in there,' I said.

Stella then lent over to her sister. 'Nana's inside there,' pointing to the coffin, and with no fear the children proceeded to identify their artwork.

'There's my butterfly!'

'There is my name.'

As the opening hymn, 'Here I Am Lord', began to play and the congregation stood, I was handed the service card.

I smiled with satisfaction. Simple and classy, I thought, so Mum. It was a beautiful picture of her and on the reverse was the poem I had written with McKenzie's drawing as the backdrop. She had included Nana and her seven grandchildren, all smiling underneath a rainbow, and the words 'I love you' were faintly written. In the top left of the card was a big bright orange sun, and scrawled in big letters under the blue sky was the word 'Goodbye'.

The full mass proceeded by the book and the kids moved around and shuffled as kids tend to do once they get bored. The priest did his bit, everyone else did theirs. Hundreds of people had come to pay their respects: family, friends, acquaintances and others I didn't recognise. They stood in line for communion and slowly filed past the bright box. Some reached out to touch it, and all of them smiled at the colourful expression of our family. Among the final few who were still in line I spotted my first boyfriend and his mother. We hadn't crossed paths many times in the last twenty years but still they had come, and the gesture prompted a surge of emotion that caught me off guard.

As we sat for the reflective prayer, the beautiful though somehow haunting song from Peter Pan was played: 'The Second Star to the Right.' We had told the children Nana was now the second star to the right, that whenever they looked up at night, she would be there. It was a little contradictory to all the effort we had made to be honest with them but we figured there had been enough reality to last them for a while.

Mary-Ann then stood and walked over to the pulpit and looked over the sea of people. 'I'd like to read a letter that Robert wrote to Pammie.' Robert and Stephen had made it clear they didn't want to speak publicly, but Mary-Ann had thought Robert's letter so beautiful she asked if she could share it on his behalf.

Mick on the other hand was determined to fight through his emotions and deliver a tribute to his mother. I had worried that perhaps our eulogies would repeat one another, until my mother's words passed through my head over and over: 'It doesn't matter.' And it didn't. 'The mistake', as we loved to call him, had memories as warm as mine but in many ways so different. To him she wasn't just his mother; from when he was eleven she had been his father too. Listening to my little brother speak made me realise how close she was to all of us. I had presumed that my relationship with her was extra-special as I was her only girl but it was evident that she had created a unique bond with each of her children.

As he sat down I stood up clutching my eulogy. My throat felt tight but my focus turned to gripping my toes tighter inside the shoe to stop it slipping off. I stood at the pulpit and looked to the packed church and took a deep breath.

Our mother was a gift. They say you don't know what you've got till it's gone ... but we knew what we had. Despite her many talents she used to tell me that the only thing she ever really wanted to do in her life was to have babies. The formal education benchmark may not have been high in our house, it still isn't, but you can't teach what this woman instinctively knew about being the best mother she could be to her four children. She would have had more if it hadn't taken Dad seven years to marry her. She had the gift of being able to create something truly special. Flowers by Pamela may have been her shop front but she was always creating something new and innovative. Anything was possible with her VISION and a glue gun. Except in the kitchen ... a great veggie soup and a roast was about it ... she did master the sponge ... but she cooked them every day for two months and it turned us off them forever.

She was a gift ... complete with the beautiful packaging ... always looked fabulously glamorous. She made sure we did too. Many would remember us as children, all perfectly matching or colour coordinated to within an inch of our lives. She had a flair for clothes, accessories, and make-up ... it was another of her art forms. As a young girl she'd say to me take that make-up off ... as I got older she'd say put more on ... and lipstick. Wear brighter lipstick. She'd flick the TV on when I was working and two seconds after the news break would go to air she'd ring with a critique. Oh I love your hair ... I think your eyes could be heavier. The news I was reading was somewhat secondary.

She had a gift for allergies. Goodness me if there was an allergy she had it. Dogs, cats, seafood, horses ... which is handy when you are married to a horse trainer ... synthetic, sulphur, rubber, and they all made her itch. As kids we'd watch TV at night on the couch and Mum would make us scratch her back ... with a knife. For a little woman, she had an unsurpassed inner strength.

When Dad was alive he was larger than life, the life of the party. She was happy for him to be that while quietly keeping the family on the slow and steady, not wanting to spoil any of the ride. She rose to every challenge before and after he died, with the amazing ability to accept her lot and move on ... embracing change, forced or otherwise.

The only equal to her love of her children ... is our children. Once the first one arrived she sold the shop to be a full-time nana ... the tally is at seven and baby Bentley is due next month. She'll be working hard now to send Michael and Haillie a baby. She said she might even send Steve and Vink another too. We agreed I didn't need any more, so instead she's going to send me a sign so I can find my lost diamond bracelet.

Grandchildren were the true joy of her later years ... spoiling them always with a lolly in her bag and constantly making skirts, headbands or pyjamas. They adored her, spending time with her. The only thing that upset Mum about death was missing out on their growth. We must work hard now to cement in their hearts what their little minds will forget. She is now the second star to the right.

I may have longed for a sister when I was younger but realised later that being the only girl allowed us a truly amazing relationship. Not many get THAT gift.

I often told people that our world didn't turn without Nana ... but of course it does and it will, though not speaking to her at the beginning and end of the day and seeing and calling her five times in between will leave an unimaginable hole. It will largely be filled with the realities of having a young family just as it was this morning at the doctor with a sick child, but for the rest of my life I will desperately miss her ... and we both knew it.

And it wouldn't have mattered when we lost her ... it was always going to hurt. It seems cruel that this round of cancer got her in fifteen months, however she'd been winning the fight for twenty-seven years and she did it for us, her children. We had known time was running out. Last year her son-in-law made it his mission to bring her closer to us. Closer than the current five minutes that is ... and he did.

To be within a few houses of her, to yell out good morning as we went to school, was never taken for granted. And while I madly and largely in vain tried to learn some of her skills in floristry, dressmaking and Christmas sacks so that I would have something to pass onto my children, the penny dropped that she'd been teaching me all along, that everything I know has been her lifelong lesson.

For years I have joked with my sisters-in-law that the jewellery would come to me ... but the most valuable was left to all of us: the sense of family, knowing the importance of it, and knowing that what looks effortless takes work. Having said that, girls, the jewellery is still mine.

Death is all part of the natural order and Mum wanted it all in order, her affairs were organised even down to us planning her funeral. 'Look fabulous,' she said. She chose the casket so that we wouldn't look cheap, and creating to the end she even sparked the idea of decorating it. I might also add she asked for a bottle of scotch to be put in there. And while I had expected for her to be dressed in one last snazzy outfit she vetoed me. 'No, I want a nightie … it's going to get awfully hot in there.'

I tried to explain death to the children a few weeks ago. One of mine summed it up, telling me that when you die they put you like in a guitar case, with a sign that says Pam is here, and then God floats you up to heaven … When I asked her a few minutes later why she was wincing she said to me I'm pinching myself so that I can cry for Nana … Mum thought that was hilarious. If only she'd heard her ask her sister last week that if she doesn't cry at the funeral could she please bite her.

Mum was gifted with a great sense of humour and it was with her till the very end. In the final week when her life had come full circle, us taking care of her twenty-four-seven ... the boys and I took turns to stay the night. Last Saturday I whispered in her ear, 'It's all done now, Mum, it's OK to go,' to which the response came: 'Go where?' The day before she said, 'I will die on Tuesday.'

For all that she gave us, all she wanted when the time came was for it to be quick and to be at home. And on Tuesday, just as she said it would be, the children she gave their first breath to ... held her and each other as she took her last . . . and that was OUR gift.

I exhaled and returned to my seat in the front pew as the priest rose, walked over to the coffin and circled around it, swinging the thurible that released the puffs of smoke from the burning incense. Regardless of the religious significance of the ritual, for me it was 'the death scent', and as a young altar girl assisting at funerals it signalled that the end was close. The final blessing for the repose of the soul of Pamela Mary Curtain was delivered, but I heard none of it; instead my focus was on three tall proud sons and one son-in-law as they walked over to the beautiful box and lifted Mum onto their shoulders.

They stood, eyes fixed straight ahead, meeting no one's gaze as the harp began to play the first few simple bars to the beautiful words of 'Perhaps Love', and then my cousin's crystal-clear voice filled the church.

I felt a crack in my armour as I watched my mother being supported by her family. The funeral director stood at the front of the box. She was holding the ring of gardenias and was beckoning me over. I didn't want to go, that's not how it was supposed to work; the order is coffin leads, family follow. She continued to wave her hand so I walked over and the ring of gardenias was placed in my hands. Oh God! How trite, I thought, but it wasn't worth resisting. It wasn't in our plan but what did it matter? I thought to myself, and we began to lead the procession out. I walked in slow steps in front of my mother, tightly holding my children's hands, Mary-Ann by my side. The tears slowly fell while I attempted to make eye contact with people and smile. We hit the fresh air and walked down the steps. The beautiful box was placed into the back of the ivy-filled hearse. It was over.

Moments later I was greeted by a blanket of bright lipsticks and words of comfort. Many women told me that they had gone out and bought a bright shade especially for Pammie. I was wrapped in hundreds of hugs but was painfully conscious that my mother was alone just a metre away. I kept one eye on the box and felt the need to stay close.

As I drowned in heartfelt condolences I saw the glass tailgate come down on the hearse. It was time. I noticed Deb the funeral director heading in my direction; we were sticking to the brief, this was where we would leave each other.

'I'm going to go with her. It's not standard practice but then nothing about this whole experience has been standard,' said Deb. Immensely grateful, I smiled and nodded. 'Thank you.'

I heard the hearse engine click over, start and then quieten to a dull hum. The windows of the shiny black car began to come down and as they lowered I heard the sounds of a big upbeat piano intro, a dramatic slide down the keys and then those familiar lyrics: 'Some girls will ... oooh, some girls won't ... oooh eee ooo.' My eyes welled as I began to chuckle and my face broke into a Cheshire Cat smile. The Racey song coming from the CD player wasn't as loud as I would have liked, and it was probably lost on most standing in the winter day, but that was OK, I did it for Mum. My job was done.

Everyone watched as the car pulled slowly out from the driveway and down the very long street in front of the church. Deb walked slowly in front of the hearse for a few metres and then got inside and the car picked up a little speed. Most people resumed chatting but I didn't take my eyes off Mum, and from various other vantage points neither did my brothers. The car finally stopped at the bottom of the small hill, turned left and out of sight. 'Goodbye Mum.'

For a split second I was caught in the middle of silence and nowhere, but it was only a moment: the kids were cold and hungry. 'Time for a drink,' said someone. 'Absolutely,' I said. As we began to walk to the car my little girls walked a few steps ahead in their twirling skirts. I reached into my bag and without even looking my hand located the familiar shape and retrieved 24K Orange: no mirror required.

Afterword

Never say never.' I actually finished something, and if you're reading this so did you, unless you are one of those people that sneak a look at the end. In all seriousness: thank you.

Six weeks after Mum died I held the inaugural Lips 'n' Sips: a small fundraiser that above all else is a reason to gather and celebrate the amazing women in my hood. The wearing of bright lipstick is compulsory. The 'sistergood' (yes my own word) is indeed a gift to all women – as are the wonderful and indelible marks we leave on each other, often without even realising it.

If you're so inclined take a look at:

 www.indeliblemarks.net

That's where you can find out more about Lips 'n' Sips as well as read stories on the incredible impact women have on one another. And for the many who wanted some photos to put to the names in the book there are a few family happy snaps there too.

Oh, and in case you're wondering, I haven't found inner peace but fate did send me on a journey not even I could have imagined.

I just miss her, I always will. The daffodils bloom each spring and 24K Orange is regularly applied. Of course I saw a psychic, but who is going to want to read about that?